MW00479866

THE DIRT ROAD

By

Phyllis JoAnn Antoine

VOLUME 1

Publishing
P.O.Box
San Diego, Ca

Publishers Stamp

All rights reserved. No part of this book may be used, stored in a retrieval system including electronically recording or reproduced in any way without written consent of the author, except in brief quotations or reviews.

Authors Notes

Any reference to actual events, real individuals living or dead or to real locations are intended only to give the novel a sense of reality and authenticity. Circumstances, names, characters, places and incidents are either the product of the author's imagination or are used fictitiously.

*To my husband and best friend Eugene
J. Antoine and all
My Children and all who made this book possible.*

Thank you

*My Granddaughter, Annie Adams for designing
the cover and photo placements*

*My daughters Beth Kadani and Vicky Antoine for editing
and formatting.*

Contents

* * *

FORWARD

It was suggested to me by my daughter Beth to call the story of my life," The Dirt Road".

A dirt road is like taking a walk with God. It offers you a quiet escape from the hectic world around you.

A dirt road can take you to a familiar place or on an adventure into unknown paths as life so often does.

Losing your way happens often in this life and there is a special joy of finding your way again. After a heavy rain, the road may be so full of pot holes that it makes it almost impassable. Many times, the curves are so sharp you can't see what is coming at you so it is hard to go on. There are times when you may just have to pull over and stop for a while and let others have the road. Sometimes the solitude of the road is interrupted by an uncaring person driving so fast and dusting you out that you can hardly see your way. There are many of these people who will touch your life too. Life is so much like a dirt road.

My dirt road is called Mother Grundy Truck Trail and Temple Trail. We named Temple Trail after Roger Temple who was one of the first old timers to live on Mother Grundy and was willing to share his dirt road and life with us. *Phyllis J. Antoine*

CHAPTER ONE- GRANDPA BAINTER'S FARM 1938-39

Grandpa Bainter's farm was in De Lassus, Missouri, not far from the county seat at Farmington, Missouri, in St Francis County. I am not sure how many acres there were but it seemed very big to me. I have no memories of actually living on the farm but I know from my mom that we did live there a short time before I was five years old.

Mostly, I remember only the visits there. I remember being at the farm for visits until I was about nine years old.

My father and mother were separated at that time. We saw very little of my father after that. We never visited my father's family or saw our grandparents again.

I remember a creek flowing through the property. My grandpa had some cows and at least one horse, probably a work horse for plowing the fields. He would put a halter on the horse and let us ride on it as he walked, holding the reins.

I remember a little calf licking my hand and how really rough its tongue felt, like sand paper.

There was a cellar where all the food they canned was kept on shelves. The cellars were pits dug into the ground with a mound of dirt over the roofs. They were always cool, even in the hot summers. We would sometimes sit in there to get cooled off. I remember they smelled very musty, sort of like moldy bread.

My grandfather seemed to me to be tall and thin. I never remember him being loving or fun. He seems to me that he was a tough old man. I don't suppose he was terribly old then, but I thought he was.

I remember riding in his car. It was an old model T, one of the first Fords made. It had only one wide long seat for two people. Behind the seat, there was a space for carrying tools. A sort of trunk. The trunk space of this model had another seat in it called a rumble seat. We never got to ride in it because it had no top on it. We would stand up behind the front seat to go for a ride.

My dad didn't have a car at that time.

Grandpa Bertram Bainter

Grandma Rhoda Bainter

My dad's mom had died when he was just three years old. His sister Lizzie raised him with her children. I guess it was too hard for my grandpa to work the farm and take care of a three year old.

My grandpa married three times. Rhoda was his third wife and that is the Grandma Bainter I remember. One day that Rhoda caught some baby mice in the cellar and she gave them to us to play with. I suppose they died or ran away.

My only other memory of the farm was the fence. It was unique. It was a wooden fence made in a zig-zag pattern of split logs. I guess I remember it because it wasn't just a straight fence like other fences were.

I also remember there was a long wooden bridge we had to cross to reach the farm. Beva, my older sister, got upset when we had to cross the bridge, because it made a lot of noise as the car ran over the wooden planks. It sounded like the planks were loose.

I guess Beva feared it would collapse.

My sister Beva and brother David did contact the Bainter family later as adults. They visited with two of my father's sisters, Aunt Hazel and Aunt Nellie.

I have a letter from Aunt Hazel to my sister Beva about the Bainter family history as Hazel remembers it.

When I was four years old, we moved from the farm into my Grandma Johnson's house (my mother's family home) in Farmington, Missouri. We lived there until I was five years old.

THE OLD BRICK HOUSE IN FARMINGTON, MISSOURI (1939-1940)

The old brick house was built for my Grandma Sallie Johnson, her husband Jimmy and family. It was built by my Great Grandfather John Henry White and my Grandfather Jimmy Johnson. The house was built on Sallie's parents' property. Sallie's mom and dad lived right next to the brick house.

My Grandma Sallie was an only child. She married my Grandfather Jimmy Johnson in Farmington, Missouri on May 27, 1906.

Grandma Sallie Johnson

Jimmy was born in Henderson, Kentucky on December 17, 1883. He died in De Lassus, Missouri on December 30, 1924. He was only forty-one years old. He worked in the lead mines of Missouri and died of what was then called miner's consumption. It was probably lung cancer or tuburculosis.

Jimmy and Sallie had twelve children, eleven that lived. All were born in De Lassus, Missouri, most probably in the old brick house.

Grandpa Johnson and Family

Children of James and Sallie Johnson

Several years after my Grandfather Jimmy died, the family stayed in the De Lassus area. When the Second World War started in Europe, my Grandmother Sallie moved to the city of

St Louis, Missouri. Jobs were easier to find there. This was probably about 1939.

My family moved into the old brick house at this time with my mom's sister and her new husband. The house was divided in half by a long hallway. On each side of the house there were two or three rooms. I think some were originally the bedrooms. On the side we lived in was the kitchen, middle room, and front room, as it was called in those days.

RUSSELL AND ELIZABETH L. BAINTER (NEE JOHNSON)
1932

Russell and Elizabeth Bainter (Dad and Mom)

We kids slept in the middle room and my parents slept in and used the front room, which was also used for company to visit in. There were four of us kids by this time, Beva, myself, Bill, and the baby, Jimmy. Mom was already expecting another baby. The back of the house had a small porch and steps going down into the yard. I guess I remember them because we played under them to get out of the sun.

There was also a cellar in the yard. It was different from the cellar on the farm. It had concrete steps and side walls that went down into it. There was a concrete ledge along the top side of it. One day I saw a caterpillar crawling on the edge of the cellar. We called these fuzzy worms or wooly worms. I wanted to show it to my brother Bill. Bill was, then, about three years old. He got too close to the edge of the cellar and fell into the stairwell. He broke his arm and I probably got into trouble for letting him fall. I don't remember but I do know there was very little money for doctors.

We had a great old family doctor, Doc Appleberry. He worked for the county and served the poor. Doc Appleberry delivered Beva, myself, Jimmy, and Sally at home.

Bill was born in Las Vegas, Nevada and David in St Louis, Missouri. Those are stories for another time. I remember Mom having to call the doctor on another occasion when Beva ran her foot through a nail protruding up through the wooden floor in the kitchen.

We were still living in the old brick house when I was almost five years old and Bill was almost four. One day we decided we could drive my dad's old Ford. Bill was standing in the driver's seat, steering the car, and I was on the floor. The starters in these cars were on the floor. As I pushed on the starter, the old car would jump forward and, of course, stop. We had no idea what the clutch was for, which probably saved us from doing real damage. Bill did not know the steering wheel steered the car. I guess he thought the faster you could turn it, the faster you would go. We ran into the trash pile where the trash was burned and we gave up driving for that day. I am sure we got a spanking when my dad saw what we had done.

Our nearest neighbors were the Kellys. They had a little girl named Mary, about Bill's age. My sister Beva and I loved to tease Bill about Mary Kelly. We would just start singing that old song, "Oh where have you been, Billy Boy, Billy Boy" and Bill would immediately run to Mom, crying. Of course, we got yelled at but it didn't stop the teasing.

BILLY BOY
Oh, where have you been, Billy Boy, Billy Boy?
Oh, where have you been, charming Billy?
I have been to seek a wife; she's the joy of my life.
She's a young thing and cannot leave her mother.

Another song my mom sang to us from this time was, "Blueberry Hill". I thought for years the mound over the cellar, was Blueberry Hill. The cellar still comes to my mind when I hear that song.

There were sad times in the old brick house too. When my brother Jimmy was only eight months old he got very sick. Doc Appleberry was no longer the county doctor. The new county doctor was not as good about coming to the house. Jimmy had always cried a lot since he was born. I remember my mom telling her sisters that one day, just to get away from his crying, she put the corner of his little gown under the heavy table leg so he couldn't wander away and get hurt and she took a walk. But it seemed no matter how far she walked she could still hear him cry. Jimmy died of double pneumonia. Mom always thought that something else was wrong with him before he got sick because he cried so much.

Mom said, too, that Doc Appleberry blamed the new doctor for not coming to care for Jimmy. In those days when a person died they didn't take you to a mortuary. The person was kept in the home for the funeral services. I remember seeing the dead baby in the bassinet in the front room. He looked like he was sleeping. I remember my mom crying all the time and the family all being there.

Later that evening, when we children were all sent to bed. We were playing around and not going to sleep. I heard someone say, "I'll give a penny to the one who goes to sleep first." I closed my eyes quickly and yelled out, "I'm asleep." I was embarrassed because everyone laughed at me. I wasn't sure why they laughed and not sure if I got the penny either.

After Jimmy died, my mom and dad seemed to be fighting all the time. These were not just arguments but actual beatings of my mom. Mom was very small, 4'11" and never weighed over 98 pounds. My dad was short, maybe 5'7", but very muscular for his size. He envisioned himself as a tough John Wayne kind of character. He had polio when he was three years old and walked with a slight limp, sort of the way John Wayne walked. He also thought he was a lady's man. He cheated on my mom right from the start of their marriage. He was a rugged handsome sort of man, as I remember.

Mom had no options but to stay with him. She had too much pride to ask for help from her family. She had only an eighth grade education and there were very few opportunities for women in those days. Even if her family was aware and wanted to help her, they couldn't. They all had families of their own to feed and care for. Many times, she would actually instigate the fights and take the beatings, hoping he would feel bad and stay home.

I remember her singing songs at these times like the "Columbus Stockade Blues." The words to this song are, "Go and leave me if you want to; never let me cross your mind. For in your heart you love another. Leave me, Darlin' I don't mind." This would immediately make my Dad angry and the fight would start.

A short time after Jimmy died, Mom was taken to the hospital. They thought she had Tuberculosis or TB. TB was highly contagious. She was not allowed to stay in our home. It turned out to be just a bad lung infection and not TB.

Joann 1940

Another memory I have of living in the brick house is of a young man named Dubart Yantzy. In my young mind, I thought he was very handsome but now I think mostly I just liked saying his name. I think Dubart was a buddy of my Uncle Ed's. I remember my Uncle Ed, who was a teenager, always hanging around our house with his buddies. He was my favorite uncle. He teased us a lot and made us cry but also made us laugh. He had an old hound dog he called "Old Judge." Old Judge was a brand of coffee back then. Mom told me later that the boys were hanging around because they knew she was about to have a baby and they wanted to be there when it came time. Mom didn't want them there, so, when her time was close she hid their horseshoes so they had no excuse to be there.

My sister Sally was born in the old brick house in August, 1940. She was the last of the family to be born there. Shortly after her birth, we moved to the big city of St. Louis, Missouri. Sally was about nine months old and Mom was going to have another baby.

* * *

CHAPTER TWO- MOVING TO THE CITY 1941-45

My father was offered a job in St Louis, Missouri by an old friend of his from Farmington, Missouri.

Mr. Chapman owned a wood and coal yard that sold and delivered these items all over the city. He needed drivers and that is what my father did for a living.

Most people used coal at that time to heat their houses, cook stoves, and water heaters, even though there were very few water heaters at that time.

Coal looked much like the briquettes we use today for our barbecue.

Children of Russell and Betty Bainter 1942

I don't remember much about our move to the city other than the apartment, which was called a flat. The building was two stories tall divided by a long hallway. There were four flats, two downstairs and two upstairs. We lived downstairs. Each flat had three very large rooms 15'x 12' with eight foot ceilings. The reason for the high ceilings was because there was no air conditioning then and the house got very hot in the summers. Of course, this made it harder to heat in the winters.

Each flat had a large kitchen, a middle room usually used as a living room but most people used it as a bedroom also. The third room was a bedroom. The kitchen had a large sink with running water. This was like a miracle to us. We had always had to carry water from a creek or well in the country and drink from a bucket with a dipper. Now we could just turn on the faucet and get a drink. There was a cook stove; some of the cook stoves had a side boiler where you could heat water as you cooked. For stoves that didn't have the attached boiler, water had to be heated in pans on the stove. Furniture consisted of a table and chairs and a cabinet. The cabinet had a bin filled with flour, with a sifter at the bottom and a counter for making bread. Most everyone made their own breads then. It had shelves for dishes and drawers for utensils. We also had electricity. The light bulbs had long pull chains on them, no wall switches yet. These were too high for us kids to reach. In the country we'd had no electricity, only oil lamps for light.

"THOSE WERE THE DAYS "

All five of us kids slept in the bedroom on one double bed. In the summer, we made pallets on the floor because it was cooler. We all bathed in the kitchen in a big tin wash tub. We heated the water on the stove. The babies were bathed first. We may have had to change the water at times. We put chairs around the tub and hung a sheet over them for privacy as we got older. Other times, we just washed up using a wash pan. We had no inside bathrooms. There was a community outhouse in the back yard. Everyone had a "chamber pot" to use at night, mostly for the kids to pee in.

We had no toothbrushes. We cleaned our teeth with salt or baking soda on our fingers. We girls learned to curl our hair by rolling it around strips of rags. This was before we could afford bobbie pins. Most days, we would get up early and go through the alleys to look for treasures people threw away in their ash pits. Ash pits were originally for dumping the ashes from the stoves but also to burn your trash in. We would look for junk to sell for spending money. We would also run errands for older people to make money for the movies etc.

There were free swimming pools in the parks we went to in the summertime. In the winter, we would ride the street cars with our student bus passes. We went all over the city. I don't think our mothers looked for us unless we didn't show up for supper.

The women were busy cleaning and doing laundry. Laundry was no easy chore. You had to heat the water, scrub every piece of clothing on a scrub board, rinse it and hang it outside on the clothes line. For some this was many trips up and down the stairs. In the winter, you hung them on a line either in the house or attic, if you had one. All the clothes had to be ironed or pressed. Most did not have electric irons then so they had to heat the flat iron on the cook stove. Ironing was almost as hard as doing the laundry. No mother would send her kids to school without pressing their clothes or with a stain on them. Pride was a big issue.

There was no television so kids got dressed and played outside most of the days. You only stayed inside if you were sick or the weather was too bad to be out. We had a big back yard to share with our neighbors. The front door opened right up to the sidewalk and street. This worried Mom a lot. She was afraid we would get out front and be hit by a car or street car. We all soon adjusted to the city life and this was not a concern. We started to play on the sidewalks with the other kids in the neighborhood. We crossed the streets many times. Most kids are very adaptable to their surroundings.

We had never had a neighborhood before moving to the city. (This reminds me of one of my grandsons, Nate, watching Mr. Rogers TV show. Nate was about three and Mr. Rogers said his opening line "Welcome to my Neighborhood". I heard Nate say, "I Yank got a neighborhood." It still makes me laugh remembering).

Our neighborhood was mixed nationalities, all white and most were poor. Very few owned a home. There were Germans, Polish, Dutch, Jews, Irish and English. Most lived close to their own nationalities. There were other sections of the city where Italians, Asians and Blacks lived. Also, nicer areas where people with better jobs and more money lived. All were segregated because of the way the U.S. was settled by immigration. Before you could immigrate to America, you had to have a sponsor or relative. You had to have a place to live. You had to speak English and have a job. You also had to be free from any disease. Most lived with their sponsor or relative at first then settled close to them in the same neighborhoods. That is how the neighborhoods and communities became segregated. It had nothing to do with not liking or hating others. The same thing happened in the freedom of the slaves. People want to be with those most like them. They stayed close to help each other. I never questioned that there were no blacks in our schools or that we lived in different parts of the city. That was just the way it was then. I do not remember ever being taught to hate anyone. We were taught the "Golden Rule" Do unto others as you would have them do unto you. Also respect anyone older than you no matter their race.

There were neighborhood grocery stores, second hand or resale stores, restaurants and a tavern on almost every corner. The taverns or bars were more like pubs. They served food and families all went to them. Only loose women went to the tavern alone until after the Second World War ended. Most women would go to the tavern and get a small bucket of beer to take home and drink it. Most businesses were all in the downtown area. All nationalities worked and shopped there together.

The first night, after we went to bed in this new place, I remember every time Mom left the bedroom and turned out the lights I got scared. There was a light that shone out from under the bed. My dad came in several times. He turned on the light and even made me look under the bed to see that there was no light there. Still, when he left the room the light came back under the bed. Finally, he came in and left the light on until I went to sleep. I was grown before I realized that the light must have come from the street light outside shining under the shade. Of course, when my dad turned off the light in the room I could see the light shining under the bed. When he would come in and turn on the light in the room, the light went away. Mystery solved. I think I still have night terrors from this and want a night light.

In the evenings, especially when the weather was hot or just nice outside, most people sat out on their front steps or stoops. This is where they would visit each other. Most never went to each other's house. Most of the men went to the tavern after dinner and visited there.

Saturdays and Sundays, we went to the movies if we had the money. Sometimes we would sneak in if we didn't have the money. Once in, you could stay all day and watch it over and over. On Sundays, the Salvation Army Band would play outside the theater. We learned all the hymns from them and the Holy Roller churches who rented empty stores for their services. We loved the music and singing and praying. Sometimes it was more entertaining than the movies. My family was not going to the Catholic Church at this time.

Bainter Family in Lyon's Park 1942

We did have radio for entertainment too. Saturday nights everyone listened to "The Grand Ole Opry." From the Opry, we learned all the words to all the country songs. From the Hit Parade Show we learned all the words to the Pop songs. Other shows we listened to were Fibber Magee and Molly, the Great Gilder Sleeve, Burns and Allen, Jack Benny, Little Theater on the Square and Inner Sanctum. No woman ever missed an episode of the soaps, like Ma Perkins and Our Gal Sunday. For the kids, there was The Green Hornet, The Lone Ranger, Batman and Robin, and, my favorite, Let's Pretend fairy tales on Saturday mornings.

One of the games we played was Rock School. Someone would hide a rock in their hand behind their back then you had to guess which hand it was in to move up the steps to the eighth grade. We also played Cowboys and Indians, Tag, Hide and Seek, Tug of War, Dodge Ball, Hop Scotch, Jump Rope, Leap Frog, Arm Wrestling, Kick the Can, Jacks, London Bridge, Farmer in the Dell, Red Rover, Colored Eggs, Blind Man's Bluff, Simon Says, Mother May I, Follow the Leader, Baseball, Marbles and so many more. We put on our own little carnivals, plays and magic shows.

We made our own toys, like rag dolls, wooden guns that shot rubber bands made from old bicycle inner tubes, shields and spears, toy sail boats, soap box cars out of wooden boxes, jump ropes made from clothes line rope, tire swings, telephones made from two tin cans and a string tied to each can, empty barrels to roll down hills or walk on and taps for our shoes out of bottle caps pushed into the soles of our shoes.

Some of the foods I remember are oatmeal served with canned milk, sugar, cinnamon and raisins. White gravy and fried bread, sort of like pancakes, sometimes biscuits, beans with ham hocks and cornbread, vegetable soups, peanut butter and imitation jelly sandwiches, chicken and dumplings and Vinegar dumplings. We would drop dumplings in boiling apple cider vinegar and sprinkle with sugar and cinnamon. We thought it tasted like cooked apples. We also ate rock candy, sugar crystalized in lard. I do not ever remember being hungry.

Mom's oldest sister Katherine and her husband Randall Boswell lived in our neighborhood also. They were about a block away on South Broadway. We called Katherine Aunt Sis. Uncle Randall was not a mean man but never very loving. He just tolerated us kids. They had no kids of their own. They had a little dog. We would go to their house to play with the dog but mostly to get cookies. Aunt Sis always seemed to have cookies.

One evening, Mom sent us all over to Aunt Sis's to spend the night. This was really something different in our lives. We never spent the night anywhere without Mom being there. The next day, Uncle Randall took us all back to our house. I remember he told us we had a new little pig there. I was so excited to see this little pig. When we reached the house, I ran into the house looking everywhere for the pig.

Mom was sitting on the bed and told us to come see the new baby. I was disappointed. There was no little pig, just this baby. We had had babies before but we never had a pig. The baby was my youngest brother David. After a while, I liked him too. He was so tiny, a runt they called him. He stayed small all his life. It was cute to be small when he was little but as he grew older, he had to deal with a lot of bullying from other boys.

We lived on Seventh Street until David was walking, about a year I guess. I was now six years old and started school at the Humboldt Public School on Sidney Street. My teacher was Mrs. Grunewald. The only thing I remember about that year was, we always had to take a nap. I hated that but did like recess.

THE CITY AND ITS SOUNDS (1940-1945)

There were very few single-family houses in the city. Some of the tenement houses were converted to single family homes. These homes were still two and three stories high. All used coal for cooking and heating. Most did not have refrigerators only ice boxes to keep food cold. Most people did not have a car so even groceries and coal and ice had to be delivered.

Very few of the houses had inside bathrooms. Most had outhouses in the backyards. If the outhouses were shared, they usually had two holes or seats. Only the children would use the outhouse at the same time. When it needed cleaning out, a man who did this job would come. He had to move the outhouse from the hole and remove the waste, I guess, with a shovel, and take it away. I am not sure where it was disposed of. Not sure who did these jobs. They were either city workers or private owned businesses. Guess his title was Pooper-Scooper. I do remember that people put lime in the outhouses to keep down the smell and maybe destroy some of the waste and kill germs. No one bought toilet paper. Not sure if there was such a thing to buy then. Money was scarce and that would have been considered a waste of money. That is probably where the old saying "Pouring money down the hole" came from. Sears gave away their catalogs for free then. Everyone had one in their outhouses. It was not only toilet paper but reading material also. Old newspapers served this purpose too. Many people learned to read in the outhouse.

Everyone had a pot, a thunder jug or slop bucket in the house to use at night. It had to be carried out and emptied in the morning. I never remember seeing a man empty the pot.

Ash Pits were also in the backyards of each house. These were made of bricks because hot ashes were emptied into them and may have had hot embers which could cause a fire. They were open pits and all burnable trash and garbage was dumped in them and burnt. The pits were cleaned out and disposed of at the dump. This was another business or job people did back then. Older kids in the neighborhoods would go through the ash pits for junk before it was burnt, to find things to sell at the junk yards. Glass and metals were being collected and used for the War effort.

Everyone was involved in the War effort then and very patriotic. Even the schools gave each kid a stamp collector's book. The kids would buy a stamp for a dime and when the book was full it was traded in for a War Bond. You kept the bond until the war ended and then could cash it in.

Collecting junk and selling it was a good way to make money for the stamps or go to the movies. It was a hard choice at times to buy the stamps. Movies only cost a nickel or a dime. We saw more movies than we had War Bonds. Now and then, our conscience would get the better of us, especially if we saw a John Wayne movie about a War Hero.

ALLEYS

Every block had an alleyway that ran behind the houses. These alleys served as emergency exits; also for delivery persons, trash collectors, the coal man, junk man and anyone who had something to sell. Each would yell out from their horse drawn wagon, cart or truck what they were selling or collecting. These were the sounds of the city. When I think back, I can still hear all the sounds the city made. It was almost musical with the vendor's yelling, the horns blowing and street cars clanging their bells. You got so used to it, you hardly paid any attention. There is an old song by Oscar Brown called "Rags and Old Iron." These are the words.

* * *

"RAGS AND OLD IRON"
Rags old iron rags old iron
All he was buying was just rags and old iron
I heard that old rag man now making his rounds
He came right to my alley lord with sorrowful sounds
Crying rags old iron and pulling his cart
Ask him how much he'd give me for my broken
heartRags old iron rags old iron
All he was buying was just rags and old iron
So, I asked that old rag man how much he would pay
For a heart that was broken baby when you went away

For a burnt out old love light that no longer beams
And a couple of slightly used second hand dreams

Rags old iron rags old iron
All he was buying was just rags and old iron
For those big empty promises, you used to make
For those memories of you that are no longer sweet
I wish he could haul them off down the street

Rags old iron rags old iron
All he was buying was just rags and old iron
When love doesn't last tell me what is it worth?
It was once mama's most precious possession on earth
When I asked that old rag man if he'd like to buy
He just shook his head and continued to cry

Rags old iron rags old iron
All he was buying was just rags and old iron

I heard that old rag man now making his rounds
He came right to my alley lord with sorrowful sounds
Crying rags old iron and pulling his cart
Ask him how much he'd give me for my broken heart

Most vendors came on a certain day of the week so everyone would have their stuff ready for them. Alleys helped to keep this traffic off the main streets. Some vendors eventually made enough money to open second hand stores or thrift stores. People did whatever they could to make a living if they didn't have an education or job.

* * *

THE RAG MAN OR JUNK MAN

The Rag man or Junk man called out, "Rags and old iron!" as he came down the alley. People gave him their old clothes for rags. Kids made spending money this way too because sometimes the rag man would give you a penny or two for the rags.

There were other vendors or sellers too that used the alleys. There were farmers selling fresh vegetables from their trucks yelling, "Vegetables! Melons!" or whatever they had that day. The tamale guy who had a cart and would yell out, "Tamales! Get your tamales! Get them while they are red hot!". The Pretzel man yelled, "Pretzel! Pretzels!. The paper boys yelled, "Post! Glove! Star Times! Paper!". Sometimes girls sold papers too. I sold newspapers and had my own corner.

These were the sounds of the city. Each vendor yelling out what he had to sell. These were the entrepreneurs of that day.

THE ICE MAN COMETH

In the summer, mostly everyone had an ice box and bought ice. Everyone had a card that had printed on it the amount of ice they wanted, from 25 pounds to 100 pounds. The ice man carried the blocks of ice to your apartment, even if it was on the third floor. Ice did not come in cubes or bags then. The ice man carried the ice with large tongs. They were big metal pointed hooks that clamped around the block of ice.

The ice man had to go to the ice house and load his truck early in the morning and deliver it before the day got too hot. All the kids followed the ice wagon and would pick up the ice that fell off on the ground.

The ice box was divided into three sections, one for the ice and one closest to the ice for food that had to stay the coldest. The last, for those that needed just to be cool. Underneath the ice box was a tray to catch the water as the ice melted. If you forgot to empty the tray you would have to mop the floor. This happened often. People went to the store for food almost every day. The refrigerator was invented for home use in 1913 but only the more affluent could afford them. They cost $700 or more in 1918. Grocery stores did have refrigeration.

THE COAL MAN

Each house had a coal bin to keep coal in. It was in the basement and usually had a window that the coal delivery man put a sort of chute into and shoveled the coal into the chute. If you didn't have a coal bin, the delivery guy would carry the coal to your apartment. Sometimes that would be up three flights of stairs. Wood or kindling was sold by the coal man too. In the winter, this was even harder, especially if the stairs were outside and icy. These weren't just six or ten steps. The houses had 8-foot ceilings so there may be twenty steps to go up.

You had to carry the coal from the basement in a coal bucket. Older people would pay a penny or nickel to the kids in the neighborhood to do this for them. This was good money. There really was penny candy then. Working in a coal yard was not an easy job. It was very dirty. The delivery guys were always covered in coal dust or soot, much like a chimney sweep. I know this was very hard for my father. He liked to dress nice and was a bit conceited. He was a hard worker, though, and well liked by his bosses and co-workers. He only did this for a short time. He later became a truck driver.

SOUTH BROADWAY

Shortly after my brother David was born, we moved again to another flat on South Broadway. It was right next to the coal yard and just up the street from Aunt Sis and Uncle Randall.

Our neighbors on South Broadway were the Deters who lived downstairs. We now had a flat on the second floor and access to the attic upstairs. The house was much the same as the flat on Seventh Street. Mrs. Deters was either a widow or a divorced lady with four kids. The oldest was a girl named Margaret who sometimes babysat us. The other three were boys, Jimmy, Tommy and Vincent. I don't remember seeing Mrs. Deters much. I guess she had a job.

The next-door neighbors were the Kellermans. They had several kids, a couple of boys about the age of my brother Bill and me. Their boys were always picking fights with Bill and throwing rocks at us. They always hit Bill in the head. Bill probably threw rocks at them also. I am sure Mom and Mrs. Kellerman had words over this. The Kellermans had a little girl about my sister Sally's age named Whimpy. Really cute little girl. I am not sure why the nick name Whimpy. There was a Popeye cartoon character in the Sunday funny papers called Whimpy who liked hamburgers. I could see nothing about him that was like this little girl. Maybe she liked hamburgers too. She certainly did not look like that character. I have one memory of Whimpy. We were singing the hymn, "Onward Christian Soldiers." There is a line in it that says, "Christ our Royal Master leads against the foe." Whimpy sang, "Christ our Royal Master leans against the floor". We all laughed at that.

Things began to change for us on Broadway, or maybe I just

hadn't paid much attention to the fights Mom and my dad had before this. I remember Mom crying a lot. I don't think she was ever happy living in the city. She had lived all her life in the same area of Farmington, Missouri. This move was very hard on her. Now, all the neighbors could hear the fighting. Sometimes Mom could not go outside because she had bruises.

There were taverns on almost every corner and most men spent their evenings there drinking. My dad did this too. Decent women still did not go to a tavern alone. But times were changing there too. The War had made a lot of changes in the way people lived. Many women went to work in the War Plants. They started going to the taverns too and drinking. Some went to keep an eye on their husbands. Many homes were broken up. Mom started going to the tavern with my dad at first. They usually got in a fight after drinking. My dad started staying away from home and had girlfriends. Some he would even take to a restaurant across the street from our house. He would come back home and tell Mom he was sorry and for a very short time things would get better. Then it would start all over again. He knew Mom would let him come back because she had no job or money to care for us. She could not make enough even if she could get a job to pay someone to babysit us. There was no welfare and even if there had been, she did not want it. She would never ask her family for help. I am sure her family were all aware of her situation. She believed if you made your bed you must lie in it. She was so full of pride. She had no money to hire a lawyer to get a divorce. Divorced women were not treated good then either.

My father and mother were first married by a Justice of the Peace, which is like a judge today. Later, my dad decided to marry her in the Catholic Church. He knew Mom and the Church did not believe in divorce. She would stay for better or worse. Mom was married for better or worse and this was the worst. No one in her family had ever been divorced. It just wasn't done.

Catholics are a funny lot. Even if they don't go to church, they still try to live by the Church laws.

MY SPECIAL DOLL

In 1943, I was eight years old and attending a Catholic School, The Assumption. This is the only time I ever went to a Catholic school. The teachers were Nuns called Sisters. They dressed in what they called Habits. These were long black dresses and black veils over a white cap that covered their heads. The cap hid all their hair. We believed they shaved their heads and wondered what they looked like without their caps on.

My Nun or teacher was named Sister Francis Katherine. She was very young and very pretty. I thought she looked like an angel. Sister's job was to teach us how Jesus would always be present in this world by performing the miracle of changing bread and wine into his body and blood at every Mass. We could receive Him into our own bodies and heart by receiving Him in the Eucharist or Holy Communion and have Him with us everywhere we went. Through our actions, that should always be Christ-like, we could show His love to all we met. He would always be with us when we needed Him. She read and told us many stories about Jesus and the lives he touched here. One story I remember was about a young boy about to make his first Communion. He was so excited and wanted this more than anything. He got very sick just before that special day and was dying. He prayed as hard as he could to get well but got no better. Just before he died Angels came to him and gave him Communion.

When it was time for me to make my First Communion, I was so excited. Sister Francis Katherine and another Nun took me downtown on a streetcar to buy me a white dress, a veil and new white shoes. Mom had no money for these things. They bought me the most beautiful white dress I had ever owned. I looked like a miniature bride. When I walked down that aisle to receive Jesus, I felt so beautiful and good. I prayed Jesus would take me straight to Heaven like he did that boy in the story. I thought I would never be that holy ever again. That was not God's plan for me and it has been really hard to always be that good again. Now I would always have to be very careful not to do anything that Jesus would not like. I did try but there were times when I wasn't always on my best behavior.

A short time after that day, Sister Francis Katherine was crossing a very busy street. It was on a very foggy morning. She was hit and killed by a streetcar. Even in her death she thought of me. The other Nuns said she wanted me to have a doll that had been very special to her. My special doll was so beautiful. She had a light blue satin dress trimmed in blue lace to her ankles. She was very old, maybe 1800's. The skirt of the dress had wire hoops to make it full. She had long ruffled blue satin Pantaloons to her ankles. She wore black patent leather shoes with buckles. Her hat was blue satin with flowers on it tied with a blue satin ribbon. I have never had a doll that beautiful again in my life. She was my most prized possession.

About a year later when I was nine years old, I got very sick. In fact, I was sick almost that whole year. First, I had the Measles, as did all my siblings. Then, I contacted Spinal Meningitis and had to go to the hospital. After surviving Meningitis, I had Diphtheria. Then, my sister Sally and I had Scarlet Fever and were hospitalized together. Each of these diseases were deadly and all contagious. There was no Penicillin yet. Each time I was sick, Mom thought I was going to die but I must have had the best doctors. She brought my doll to the hospital to comfort me when I had Meningitis. The doll had to be burnt because it had become contaminated and might carry the disease to others. That broke my heart but I have my memories of someone who loved me a lot.

I have one memory of sharing my birthday that year with my dad. He took me and a friend to a movie. I remember him walking to the theater and paying for our tickets but don't remember him staying for the movie.

There were other memories of Broadway.

The main one was the day World War ll ended in Europe. I was on the street playing with other neighborhood kids. Suddenly, the whole city went crazy. People came running into the street, out of their houses and out of the stores. Some were screaming, some were crying, some laughing and some yelling, "It's over! It's over!". Everyone in cars were blowing their horns. The streetcars were all clanging their bells and fire engines set off their sirens. I was absolutely terrified. I thought the world was coming to the end. I ran for my house crying and knew everyone would be gone.

Of course, Mom knew it was the war that had ended and got us all calmed down. I will never forget that day. I was totally scared.

THE SEPARATION

I remember the last fight Mom and my dad had. It was the day the War ended. Everyone was out celebrating and drinking. Mom and my dad were separated. Mom went to the tavern across the street to celebrate with some of her friends. My dad showed up there and told her to go home, not that nicely. She refused and he pulled her outside and started to beat her. She got free from him and ran home. We were all in bed and heard her come in and slam the door and lock it. My dad was right behind her. He kicked the door open. We ran into the room to see what was going on. Mom ran to the window. This was on the second floor, about fourteen feet high. We were all screaming at her not to go out the window. She climbed out and hung on to the window sill, then she fell. My dad ran back down the stairs, leaving us all there stunned. We looked out the window but she was gone.

Not sure about the time but she did come back the next day. Life went on from there. It wasn't discussed, but it was different. That fight was the end of their life together. My dad never came back after that.

The war had changed society, not just our lives. Women started working in war plants building aircraft and things needed for the war. Women became more independent. Many of them had husbands in the war and felt they could help them by building airplanes etc. Women started wearing slacks or pants. I think this was because it was easier to work in but it also made them feel stronger and more able. Dresses became something you wore to church or for special occasions.

When the men returned from the war, many came back different. Many had problems adjusting to the changes and women being so independent. They did not like all the changes. Women had gotten used to taking care of the family without the men. Divorces became commonplace when it had been almost a disgrace before the war. Now it was acceptable.

Mom did finally go to work in a cookie factory. We were able to manage without my dad for the first time. My sister Beva was twelve now and she was our babysitter when Mom worked. It was fine until one day when David, age four, was outside unattended. A policeman brought him home. When he found out Beva was only twelve and Mom was working, he went to the factory and made Mom come home. He told her she had to hire a babysitter or quit work. This was the worst time for Mom. She did not make enough to hire a sitter and could not quit her job or we would starve. That was the straw that broke the camel's back. I guess this saying came about because a camel could carry so much and people just kept piling it on.

Shortly after the police made Mom leave her job, we went to Farmington to her sister Mabel's house. Someone must have driven us there, probably Aunt Sis and Uncle Randall.

THE ORPHANAGE

I am not sure any of us knew what Mom had in mind that day in May 1945. I think she was not sure herself. We thought we were just going for a walk around town with her. There was a Presbyterian Orphanage in Farmington, the town where she had grown up. Mom took us to the Orphanage. We entered the front door and an older woman met us. We later knew her as Mrs. Bascum.

The Orphanage looked like a school building. Mrs. Bascum took Mom in the office while we waited in the hall. When she came out of the office, Mom told us we would have to stay there for a while. She would come and get us as soon as she could. She had to get a better job so she could take us back with her.

An older man came out of the office and introduced himself, "My name is Mr. Walker I am the superintendent here and Mrs. Bascum is my assistant. You are all going to be staying here for a while with us until your mom can take you home again." Mom kissed us all good-bye. We all held on to her for as long as we could but we older kids had to try and calm down David and Sally. They had never been away from Mom before. None of us had ever been away from Mom.

Bainter family the day they went to the orphanage. Farmington, MO, 1945

David and Beva Bainter at the orphanage in Farmington, MO, 1945.

After Mom left, Mrs. Bascum took us each to different dormitories; Beva to the house next to the main building for girls thirteen and over, Bill to another building for middle sized boy. David was on one end of the main building for little boys and Sally on the other end for little girls. I was upstairs in the main building for middle sized girls. We were told we would see each other at dinner in the dining hall.

I was introduced to our house Mother, Mrs. Rainey. She was a nice lady. She showed me a bed that was to be mine. She handed me the sheets and had me make the bed. I think she was impressed that I knew how. I had learned to make beds when I was in the hospital the year before. The nurses would let us help them. There were no fitted sheets in those days so when I knew how to fold the corners of the bottom sheet Mrs. Rainey was surprised. After I finished making the bed, Mrs. Rainey took me to a large closet. The closet had shelves that were divided into squares called cubby holes. Each child had a cubby hole for their socks underwear, pajamas and play clothes. They were all folded neatly. We each had our own locker for our hang-up clothes, coats etc. I was given five dresses. Three were for school. You wore one on Monday and Wednesday, one on Tuesday and Thursday and one on Friday.

When you came in from school, you were to change into your play clothes and hang up the dress you wore that day. The other two dresses were for Sundays and special occasions. Every child had a sponsor, a family that bought your shoes, clothes, birthday gift and Christmas presents. I think they were all the members of the Presbyterian Church across the street from the orphanage. This would be the church we would go to now. We never knew our sponsors or met them.

I was also shown where the clean sheets were kept and told we were to change our sheets once a week on Saturday. We had chores to do on Saturdays also.

We had to clean the bathroom, sweep, mop, and wax the dormitory floors, dust our areas and make sure it was always straight and clean. Every morning before breakfast, we were to make our beds. There were about twelve girls in my dorm. Six beds on each side of the room.

After getting all these instructions, I was sent to the bathroom to bathe and change my clothes. I never saw my clothes again. I guess they were thrown away. After my bath, Mrs. Rainey gave me a toothbrush and toothpaste. She told me to put the toothpaste on the brush then brush my teeth. I never had a toothbrush before this. I put lots of the paste on the brush. Mrs. Rainey looked into the bathroom and said very loudly, "Oh my God! You have enough toothpaste on that brush to kill a horse!" Well, I took almost all of it off the brush and from then on, I used just a dab. I wasn't putting anything that was strong enough to kill a horse in my mouth ever again. In fact, I hardly used toothpaste again. I just used water. When we were done with all that, I was taken back downstairs to Mrs. Bascum. She told me I was to have my hair cut very short. All the girls had to have the same short haircut. I had just learned to braid my hair. I cried and begged her not to cut it. I told her I could take good care of it and would keep it braided. She would not listen to me. She repeated all the girls must have their hair short because they might get lice. It was easier to get rid of lice with short hair. I had had lice before so I knew this was true. I still begged her not to cut my hair. Mrs. Bascum then threatened to spank me if I didn't stop crying. So, my hair was cut. I hated the haircut and Mrs. Bascum. I guess she was the first person I ever hated in my life. But I did hate her.

(Digression: I had a chance to go to college in my forties and took a creative writing class. I wrote the story of my haircut. I thought I had dealt with that trauma in my life way back then but I had all the emotions of that ten year-old girl as I wrote the story, all the pain and realization that it was not just my hair I had lost that day. I had lost my father, Mom was gone and could not comfort us. My sisters and brothers were all living in different areas or houses. Even our clothes were taken from us and then, "Last Straw" was my hair. I had absolutely nothing left of my life as I had known it from my birth. It was the most shattering experience I had ever had to deal with and I had to deal with it alone. No one had done any of this to me to be mean. Still, they could never know how awful that day was for me and my siblings. I am sure they each had their own story to tell and deal with too).

As the hours became days and days became weeks, weeks became months. We grew to accept all the changes as our way of life. We hoped that Mom would soon be able to come and get us. In the meantime, we just looked forward to the Sunday visits when Mom could come. She came as often as she could. It was very difficult for her, even dangerous at times. She had no extra money for buses and had no car. It was over eighty miles to the Orphanage from St Louis. She would start out very early on Sunday morning taking the streetcar to the end of the line. From there she would walk and hitch hike rides with anyone who would stop and pick her up. Sometimes the men who picked her up would make passes at her and she would be forced to get out of their cars and hope for another ride.

Once, she was picked up by a truck driver who wasn't supposed to pick up people. He was hauling cars so he had Mom ride in one of the cars on the truck.

We looked forward to her coming so she made the sacrifices willingly. She loved us more than anything else in life. She wanted to be with us and she said that in her poetry. She was a good poet and writer. All of her poems and writings were about us and her life. She said her writing was her therapy.

I later had her poems copyrighted and put in a book called "The Value of Life" for all my siblings to share. She would sometimes put music to the poem and sing them to us. One was the lullaby she sang to us and we have all sang to our children and grandchildren called "Little Sleepyhead."

LITTLE SLEEPYHEAD
By BETTY BAINTER (AKA) VIRGINIA JOHNSON

Little Sleepyhead, it's time your prayers were said
It's time for you to tumble into bed
I know the Sandman is around by your sleepy sigh
So cuddle close while mother sings to you a lullaby
While the moonbeams chase the shadows
And the stars play peek-a-boo
Take a dreamy trip on the Sandman's ship
And sail the whole night through
Sail away, sail away, to the land of dreams
While Angels guard your bed
He will bring you back to me at dawn
Lullaby and goodnight Sleepyhead.

Another poem written at that time was titled, "My Five Little People"

MY FIVE LITTLE PEOPLE
By BETTY BAINTER

My Five little people, I miss having around
Five little voices, I miss hearing their sound.
Five hungry mouths I miss at meal time
Five pairs of feet that were never on time.
Five little faces I miss night and day
Five little people, I miss hearing them pray
Five pair of arms that clung to me tight
I miss them all so when retiring at night
Five little people with a hard way to go
Take it like troupers the grandest I know
For their hearts like mine are breaking inside
At being apart yet they seldom have cried
Five little people trying hard to be Gay
Five little hearts plan for the day
And I'm hoping and praying the time will soon be

When my five little people are back home with me

Mom was not taking good care of herself. Her health had not been good since Jimmy's death and had gotten worse after the births of Sally and David. All this was taking a toll on her but she was a fighter and would not give up. One Sunday, a man who had been fishing picked her up and, after hearing her story of why she was hitch hiking, felt sorry for her. He started showing up several times. After a while, he just started bringing her to visit us as often as he could. His name was Fred Bailey. We were told to call him Uncle Buck. Guess it made it seem he was more related to us.

DIGRESSION:
(I want to digress here again to an important happening that is important to my story. Mom's family had always been Catholic. Mom had quit going to church when she married my dad, but when tragedies happen such as a death of a child most return to their Faith and Church. When Jimmy became ill, Mom wanted him Baptized and sent for the Priest, Fr Dirker came. He not only Baptized Jimmy but all of us, after Mom and my dad agreed to go back to Church. I was not aware of all this until I was grown. I thought we were all baptized as babies.

I was talking to Mom one day and I asked her why Fr Dirker had given me Communion before I made my First Communion. I had remembered it tasted like salt and Communion does not taste salty. That was when she told me it was at my Baptism. Salt was a symbol of incorruption (free from physical decay) and to sustain life. Salt was always used to preserve food and keep it from rotting. Communion is also to sustain life of the soul).

As time passed, we adjusted to the separations.

We were able to see each other on the way to school, out in the play yard and at dinner in the dining hall. On Sundays, we walked across the street for church and Sunday school. This was my first experience of Sunday school and I really liked it. They read and told us stories from the Bible. We learned many hymns. On Sunday evening, we had what they called Junior Christian Endeavor classes where we had to memorize verses from the Bible and had Bible study. I really liked these classes.

This is where my Baptism becomes so important to me even though I did not know it then. I mentioned that I had felt as though I had nothing left of my life as I had known it before coming to the Orphanage. Then I realized that I had one more thing. I was a Catholic and, try as they may, they could not make me a Presbyterian. Later in my life, I would investigate the Faith and really choose to be a Catholic but, had it not been for my Baptism, that may never have happened.

We started school and we could walk together to school. Some of our cousins went to this school. We enjoyed knowing there was family in town. Although, I never remember them coming to the orphanage to see us.

Life was different but it really wasn't bad. It was the first time I ever had my own bed and had three meals a day. We slept in a dorm but you had your own space. We could listen to the radio while we cleaned the dorm on Saturdays. One other favorite radio show was "The Hit Parade". It was the ten best songs or top hits for that week.

There was also a magazine called "Hit Parade" which printed all the words to these pop songs and told about the people who sang them. This was my favorite thing to read. We learned all the words to the songs.

CHRISTMAS 1945

That year around Christmas time, our dad came to the orphanage to see us. Christmas must have put a guilt trip on him. This was the only visit I remember. He asked what we wanted for

Christmas. I told him I wanted to have my hair permed. I was still angry at having my hair cut. I guess he talked to Mr. Walker or Mrs. Bascum because they agreed to let me go to the local beauty shop and get the perm. I think it cost ten dollars which my dad had given me for Christmas.

To get a perm in those days, your hair was rolled onto rollers. Then, they had a chair that looked like an electric chair. It had many clips on the ends of wires that were clipped to each roller. After I got my perm and paid for it with my Christmas money, the beauty shop decided they would give free perms to all the girls at the orphanage that wanted them.

That Christmas was the first year dolls were made with what was called magic skin. It was a rubber base and felt like real skin. Before this, dolls were either rag dolls are made of hard plastic. My sponsors gave me a magic skin doll. I loved that doll. This was the first and only Christmas I had ever gotten what I asked for.

As I said before, Mom came as often as she could and we all looked forward to that. After a short time, Mom came and took Beva home with her. I think Beva took some potato chips from the kitchen where she had a job helping with meals. This was considered stealing. It was embarrassing for Mom. I am sure that is why she took Beva with her. It was also because Mom was so lonely and Beva was twelve and able to be at home alone after school so the police would not get involved.

THE RUN AWAYS

After Christmas and Beva leaving the home, some of the girls in my dorm decided they would run away. I planned to go with them. I don't know where we thought we would go. I may have been upset that Mom took Beva home with her and left the rest of us. I don't remember being mad but I may have been. As things turned out I didn't get to go with the girls.

When the girls did run away I was in a different dorm. Sally, who was five at this time, was having some problems adjusting to her dorm. Mrs. Brown, her supervisor, thought it would help her if I was there with her. She asked that I be transferred to the little girls' dorm to help the younger ones get ready for their baths and bed. In the mornings, I made sure they brushed their teeth and got ready for school and church. I was happy to do this.

The runaways only got about six miles from the home. They were found and brought back and kept in isolation as a punishment for about a week. We were not allowed to talk to them. Eventually they were allowed to eat in the dining room again. The first evening we made eye contact. I must have smiled at one of them. We may have even giggled. At any rate, whatever happened made Mrs. Bascum mad at me and she made me go into her office. She told me I was encouraging the girls to run away again. She made me bend over a chair and hit me a couple of times with a belt or strap. I was so angry and vowed to myself that she would never do that to me again.

I hated her for that because I was sure I had done nothing wrong.

On my way to school, I told my brother Bill and a friend of his Carl that I was writing to Mom to come and take me home too. I didn't have a stamp to mail the letter. Bill said he and Carl would steal a stamp from the office for me, which they did somehow. We knew if I mailed the letter from the home Mrs. Bascum would read it. I mailed the letter on the way to school and one of the girls I thought was a friend saw me do it. She threatened to tell Mrs. Bascum unless I gave her my new doll. I gave her the doll and she told on me anyway. I was immediately moved back upstairs to the other dorm as punishment.

I was not trustworthy to stay with the little girls. Mrs. Rainey the supervisor of the middle-sized girls was very nice to me. She asked why I had mailed the letter myself instead of talking to someone about being unhappy. She didn't punish me any further.

A few weeks after that letter, Mom came and took us all home with her even though she really had no room for us to be with her.

BACK IN THE CITY ON CASS AVENUE 1946

Mom, Beva and Uncle Buck came to the home to pick us up and take us to our new home. We drove to St Louis and Uncle Buck dropped us off at a big three story building. Mom called it a rooming house. People that lived there had only one room to sleep in and live in. There were no bathrooms in the rooms. Each floor had a bathroom in the hallway that everyone used or shared. The building was very old and in a rundown area of the city.

We gathered our bags of belongings, told Uncle Buck thank you for the ride and help. We said our good byes and entered the building. It was a very dark entryway with a flight of stairs going up to the second floor where Mom's room was. Mom showed us the bathroom and told us when we used it to be sure we locked the door and not to play around in there. Others had to use it too. It was shabby looking and not too clean. If the bathroom was occupied, we had to go to the filling station (gas station) on the corner and they would let you use the bathroom there. We did this often because the filling station bathroom was cleaner than the one in the rooming house.

Mom unlocked the door to her room. Inside there was an old double bed. Beds then did not have box springs and plush mattresses like the beds do today. The headboard and foot were made of metal tubing they were connected by two metal railings on the sides to fasten the head and foot together. Across the railings there were four or five wooden slats and the metal springs laid on the slats. Then the mattress was placed on the springs. Mattresses were crudely made of cotton batting and after some use they tended to get very lumpy when the batting would separate. If the slats weren't measured just right it was not uncommon for them to move and the springs to fall off the railing.

When Mom took the room, there was just her living in the room. Then she shared it with Beva and now we all were there.

We all had to sleep on this bed so instead of laying on the bed normally we would have to sleep across it. Thank God, we were all small even Mom. She was 4'11. There were two old chairs and a small wooden table. Sometimes Mom would push the chairs together and sleep on them to make more room on the bed. Sometimes one or two of us would wind up on the floor. It was as comfortable as the bed.

There was a small electric hot plate, like one burner on a stove, we used to cook on; also, an old dresser. A dresser was a chest of drawers with a big mirror attached to it. We had a mirror but it had a long crack down the center of it.

Beva dresses up with mop-wig. St. Loius, MO, 1946

After a few weeks, we adjusted to this new place. We started back to school. We were happy to go to school and have some-place to go where there were clean bathrooms. The school was nicer than staying in the room and listening to the radio, which was our only entertainment.

We were lucky enough to have a radio. The music and the pro-grams were a good escape from the real world, especially for Mom. Music always makes life more bearable. I don't remember being unhappy there. We were all so happy to just be together again in our own place.

We got familiar with the neighborhood and ran the streets. We made friends with other kids in the neighborhood that were as poor as we were. Sometimes we just went for walks and window shopping in the stores. Woolworths, called a Dime store was like the 99 cents or dollar stores of today. We had no money but we would go in and look around and hope someday to be able to buy something. Bad idea.

One day when Bill and I were in Woolworths, I saw some finger-nail polish. It was on sale for two pennies. We each took some, shoved it in our pockets and left the store with it. I still wonder why we stole this finger nail polish. We had absolutely no use for it and certainly could not bring it home. Mom would want to know where we got it. I don't remember what we did with it, guess we threw it away.

Bill got a small job selling papers on a corner. I would do his job if he didn't want to. Sometimes we would both work the corner. Eventually, he got a regular paper route and I took his corner. Beva looked after Sally and David while mom worked at the cookie factory. I think Mom made a little over ten dollars a week and our rent for the room was ten dollars a week. There was very little left over for food and other necessities. Not sure how Mom managed to feed us, but she did.

One day, the landlady came to our room to talk to Mom. It was not a good visit. Mom had not told her about our being there. She told Mom she was not allowed to have all those people in that one room. It was against the law, but, if Mom would con-sent to cleaning the bathrooms and the stairwells once a week, the landlady would let us stay there. Mom was not well and doing this cleaning and working was not something she could do. She told the landlady she could not do this. So, we were told we would have to move. I remember Mom looking for another place, even a garage. This is another poem in her book, "Value of Life", "No Children Allowed". When she told anyone she had five children, they would not even consider renting to her, espe-cially since she had no husband. Single moms were not common then and divorce was almost unheard of.

"NO CHILDREN ALLOWED"
By BETTY BAINTER

Every time I had seen a 'For Rent' sign, I would
ask about renting the place
As soon as they knew there were children, they
would just close the door in my face

Many miles I had walked through the city, trying
to find us a place to call home
A garage or in somebody's attic, would've beat living
down in the slums

Cats and dogs live in nice places, are protected
and pampered for years
While children must live in the ghettos, unprotected
and surrounded by fears

Growing weary from all the rejections, I
gave up and moved to the park
Where Newspaper Jim and the Captain, came
to help before it was dark

So, the newspapers carried the story, but I never had a regret
Because it helped others just like us, and I hope
those landlords, never forget

I salute those two angels of mercy, the Captain and Newspaper Jim
For the kindness and friendship, they offered,
when my world seemed hopelessly grim

SALSBURY PARK 1947

When Mom finally got very desperate, she took her next ten
dollar pay check and hired a man with a truck to take the few
boxes of our belongings to a park near where her mother lived,
Salisbury Park.

She paid the man six dollars and with the rest of the money, she took us on the bus to the park. When we got there, the man unloaded our boxes by a bench and left. Mom sat on the bench as we enjoyed the park swings and playing. I suppose Beva was the only one aware of the anguish Mom was going through. The rest of us had no idea what was going on.

Every neighborhood had a beat cop then. Each policeman or cop had several blocks he walked called his beat. Everyone knew their policeman. He was part of the neighborhood. He knew all the kids by name and where they lived. He knew their moms and dads. There was no fear of the policeman. He was your friend and you were always to go to him if you were lost or hurt. You were always respectful to the policeman and any adult because they knew your parents and if you embarrassed your parents you were in real trouble.

Manners were instilled into everyone, rich or poor. You were taught respect for any adult. You never even thought about talking back to someone older than you, not even store clerks or streetcar drivers. It just wasn't done.

While we were in the park, the policeman had walked by us several times throughout the day. He talked to us and spoke to Mom. I am sure he wondered about the boxes but probably thought we were waiting for someone to come and get us. I guess that is what we thought too.

It started to get dusky towards the end of the day and the policeman came again. This time he asked Mom if someone were coming to get us.

She finally told him, "No." We had nowhere to go. She wanted to sleep on the benches just for the night and would look again in the morning for a place to stay. He told her that was impossible and she would have to find someone to come now. She could not be in the park after dark. At this point she was so desperate and said we could not and would not leave the park. The policeman went away, but shortly after he left, another policeman and several other people came.

Some were reporters from the local newspaper, The Post-Dispatch. Of course, the people who lived around the park came too. Seeing all the police they were curious also. After several arguments, some of the people, realizing how desperate Mom was, offered to take us into their homes for the night. The police chief was very compassionate and promised he would help Mom all he could to find a place for us.

I am quite sure Mom never gave a thought to the fact that the authorities could have taken us away from her and put us in an orphanage again.

The next day our dad came. He met with Mom and the police chief and claimed that he was not aware of our situation until he had seen the newspaper story. Also, he said that he had sent money to Mom for our care but she drank with it. All this, of course, were lies. He sent no money. He said he had no place to take us either.

Family Of 5 Found In Park Gets Home In Household Of 6

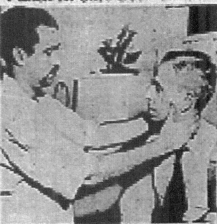

Sinatra Fells Writer With Punch In Cafe Over 'Insult'

AFTER THE BATTLE a doctor looks over Columnist Lee Mortimer.

AMAZING! THE Magic Slip

The St. Louis Star and Times (St. Louis, St. Lo

same article enlarged

ST. LOUIS STAR-TIMES
10 — Wed., Apr. 9, 1947.

Family Of 5 Found In Park Gets Home In Household Of 6

Mrs. Betty Bainter and her five children, who set up housekeeping in Hyde Park Monday, today had a roof over their heads, thanks to Mr. and Mrs. Nicholas R. Miranda, 1408A Montrose av.

Although they have four children of their own, Mr. and Mrs. Miranda invited the Bainter family to share their small three-room flat until the Bainters find a home of their own.

Police Capt. John A. Buck of the Penrose st. district reported his station has been swamped with telephone calls from individuals and welfare agencies anxious to help the Bainters, who reported they were evicted from their single room when Mrs. Bainter objected to paying half of her $20 weekly earnings for rent.

Buck stated one woman drove to the police station in a limousine and offered to pay six months' rent in advance in any apartment the family could find and also offered to provide furnishings for an apartment if necessary.

The Salvation Army also offered to help but stated it could not shelter the family in its mission because only one bed was available there.

Mrs. Bainter's husband, Russell, appeared at the prosecuting attorney's office yesterday and stated he had lost track of his family after they moved from a previous address and did not know their whereabouts until he read in the papers of their eviction. He was referred to Capt. Buck, but Buck said this morning that Bainter had not yet appeared at the police station.

Newspapers by ancestry   The St. Louis Star and Times (St. Louis, St. Louis, Missouri) · 7 Apr 1947, Mon · Page 11

Downloaded on Mar 4, 2019

Mother And Five Children Set Up Housekeeping In Park

A 34-year-old mother and her five children set up housekeeping in Hyde Park this afternoon after she reported being evicted from their single third-floor room in a rooming house.

With pasteboard boxes and tubs containing clothing, kitchen utensils and odds and ends of personal possessions cluttered around her, Mrs. Betty Bainter sat on a bench in the park, at 20th and Salisbury sts., and related her troubles to reporters and sympathetic bystanders as her children played on the grass.

Making only $20 a week in a bakery, Mrs. aBinter said she objected to paying $10 a week rent for the one room in the 1400 block of Cass av., particularly as she had runing water only infrequently and was unable to keep the children clean.

However, the landlady refused to reduce the rent and Mrs. Bainter said she was ordered to move today when she declined to pay the regular $10 rent. She chose Hyde Park "because that's the only park I know." When she saw an empty truck passing, she hailed the friendly driver and he hauled her meager possessions to the park.

Mrs. Bainter said she and her husband have been separated for a year and she does not know his whereabouts. They came to St. Louis six years ago from Farmington. The children are Beva, 13 years old; Joan, 11; William, 10; Sally, 6, and David, 5. Frank L. G. Weiss, proprietor of the Union Hardware & Mercantile Co., 1428 Salisbury st., was canvassing the neighborhood late today trying to find a place for the family to sleep tonight.

World Federation Group To Meet Here

Approximately 300 supporters from 15 states will convene in St. Louis Friday and Saturday for the first Midwestern Conference on World Federation. Highlighting the program Friday night will be addresses by Seldon Waldo, Gainsville, Fla., president of the U. S.

After he left, the police chief said he had found a family that would let us stay with them until we found a place to live and he knew a lawyer that would help Mom get a divorce. Then she would qualify for Aid to Dependent Children or (ADC) as it was called then, now known as Welfare. This was only available if you were divorced. Being Catholic, she didn't believe in divorce but now she had no choice.

We moved into an apartment with a man and his wife for a few days. Then, we were moved into an apartment of our own on Chateau Ave. We started school again. Life seemed to get better.

Mom continued to see Uncle Buck. He would come and take us on picnics and fishing trips on the weekends. He was older than Mom. He was a little heavy and sort of balding. He always wore a suit coat and hat. He looked like a business man except when we went camping and fishing. He still wore the dress hat even then, never a baseball hat. He was a very talented man. I remember he made an electric guitar from a piece of cedar wood for one of my uncles. He could build a house from the ground up and remodeled most of the old houses we would live in.

Once he made a ship out of Plastic with people and an engine that he would sail on the lake, it was remote so he could guide it from the shore. It was beautiful.

On one of our fishing trips to Creve Coeur Lake, Uncle Buck found an abandoned cabin. It had been in the flood and I guess who ever owned it didn't want to fix it up again. There were four or five cabins there, all deserted and needing repair. Uncle Buck was a roofer and worked in the building trades.

Cabin at Creve Couer

He somehow bootlegged electricity to the cabin. We spent days cleaning mud out of it. He made it livable and we moved into it. He drove a metal pipe into the ground until it hit water. He put a hand pump on the pipe. The water had lots of iron and rust in it. It didn't taste too good but he was sure it was safe to drink if we boiled it. We did and drank it for the next three years we lived there and were all healthy. I guess he was right. There was no inside plumbing so he built us an outhouse.

Uncle Buck didn't live with us at first but he finally asked Mom to marry him and she did. They were married by a Judge in Leadwood, Missouri when we went to visit Mom's sister, Aunt Mary. After that, Buck lived with us at the cabin except when his work took him out of town or when he and Mom were fighting. He had no children of his own but we would find out later that he was married.

One day after they were married, Mom was going to send Buck's suit coat to the cleaners. She was checking to make sure there was nothing in the pockets. In the inside pocket, there was an envelope from the IRS. It was his tax return but it did not have Mom's name on it as his wife. It had an Ethel Bailey as his wife. There was a big fight and Uncle Buck packed his things and left the cabin. I think Uncle Buck wanted a family so bad he was willing to marry Mom to get it. This was also why we never lived any place where we had to pay rent so there would be no paper trail.

One morning, shortly after this incident, Mom was outside sweeping off the concrete slab that once was a patio. A man drove up and got out of his car and walked up to her. Not sure what he said but the next thing we saw was Mom chasing the guy with the broom trying to hit him. He was running to get back into his car.

All of a sudden, our neighbor's goat Nellie got excited and started chasing Mom. Mom was scared of the goat so she also got into the man's car. He told her he was a lawyer; his name was Phil Finger. He showed her some divorce papers from Ethel. After that incident, Uncle Buck returned. We never got the whole story about Ethel.

Bill & Joann with Pig

We had a good life at the lake cabin. It was a great place for us kids. We could fish in the lake, no licenses needed, no game wardens. We hunted rabbits and squirrels with the 22 rifle Uncle Buck gave to Bill. We worked for a farmer who had fields next to the lake, for spending money. We made twenty-five cents for a crate of cut spinach. This was not easy money. The work was hard. To cut spinach, you must crawl along the rows and cut it

off at the ground. After the fields were harvested, we could collect the vegetables that were left in the fields. Some things grew
wild like asparagus and other greens, as they were called. We
also planted gardens so we were never hungry there.

Uncle Buck also built us a small barn and brought us a mule.
We named her Judy. Later, we would learn all female mules are
called Judy. We thought Judy was a horse and rode her bare back.
We had no saddle, just the reins. For Judy's sake and to stop arguments about whose turn it was to ride her, Uncle Buck made us
a wagon so we all could ride, especially the smaller kids. He also
got us a bike to share.

Naturally, we all wanted it at the same time too. Beva being the
oldest got first rights. Bill and I were happy to share but could
only have the bike if Beva let us. We would ride together or take
Sally or David for a ride since they were too small for a two-
wheeler.

Beva @ Cabin @ Cleve Couer Mo
1947 coal hiding wood Pile for
cook stove.

Beva in Cabin at Creve Couer

On many occasions, we would give Mom a ride to town. The town of Creve Coeur was about five miles from the lake. Mom told me once she was a little embarrassed, but more embarrassed when other kids would ask her if she wanted a ride. She never learned to ride a bike herself. Once, when I was giving Bill a ride, he somehow got his foot caught in the fork of the front wheel. We were both thrown off the bike. It was hard and painful getting Bill's foot loose. We had no tools to take the wheel off. We just kept twisting his foot until it came loose. Luckily no broken bones. Riding double on a bike is never a good idea.

With the little bit of money we made picking spinach, etc., we could go to the movies occasionally. This was a real adventure. We had a john boat for fishing so we could row across the lake to a place called the Chain of Rocks Park. We would tie up the boat and climb a long set of stairs to the top of a hill where the streetcars would turn around and go back to the town of Overland. It was about a twenty minute ride to the theater. After the movie, we would take the streetcar back to the park, get the boat and row across the lake to home. Sometimes it would be dark and a little scary.

We had pets even though we hardly had food enough to feed ourselves. We had a couple of stray cats and two little dogs, Tina and Tim.

Joann with dogs

One of our neighbors, Albert Mayo shot the mother of the puppies because she was getting into his chicken house and sucking the eggs. It was his living and he said you could never stop a dog from doing this once they start. I remember following him and begging him not to shoot the dog but he would not listen to me. It was a very traumatizing thing to see. I thought he wouldn't shoot her if I was there but he did.

Albert was only sixteen. He was a good boy. His family had moved into one of the cabins at the lake. His family was as poor as we were. His father was in prison for stealing a cow to feed his family. Albert raised chickens for food for his family and to sell. He also sold the eggs. He helped his mom raise the other four kids.

FERN RIDGE SCHOOL

We really did walk three and half miles to school and this is not an exaggeration. We did this in snow and rain. We were not lucky enough to have gloves and rubber boots or goulashes, as they were called back then. Sometimes, we had gloves but mostly we kept our hands in our pockets. Mom never made us go to school if the weather was bad and cold. I do remember how my hands would hurt when they started to warm up and the blood returned. I think we were close to frost bite many times. We would stand by the radiator in the classroom to thaw out. I always wondered why they didn't have school when the weather was nicer; but then, we probably would not have gone if it was too nice outside.

Our school at Fern Ridge was a one room school. Mrs. Graham, our teacher taught all eight grades when we first came to this school. She taught even numbers one year and odd the next. I had gone to fifth grade and was lucky to start when she was teaching sixth. If you were going into fifth grade that yea,r she either put you up or back according to how you could do the work.

Mrs. Graham was the best teacher I have ever met in my life. She had no children of her own and treated each of us as her own. She not only taught us our lessons, she taught us baseball, games, music, manners and health. I remember when the three of us girls in sixth grade pierced our ears. We just took a large needle and dipped it in alcohol and pierced the ear lobe and put in the wires. Of course, we had some infection and soreness. Mrs. Graham cleaned our ears and medicated them until they healed. She bought peroxide and whatever we needed. She nursed us when we had colds, pierced our ears, etc. She also spanked those who needed it. She never called our parents because most of them did not have phones or cars to get to the school.

There were six kids in my class that first year at Fern Ridge School. Four boys, Dennis, Roger Hummel, Eddy Dauster and Silvio Lombardi and two girls, myself and Charlan Deitz. The next year, a new girl came named Wanda Turrentine. Wanda was beautiful, dark hair and olive skin. She had developed early so she made Charlan and I look very plain and boyish. All the boys had a crush on Wanda. Charlan and I didn't want to like her at first. A little jealous, I guess; but, as time went by, we all became great friends. Wanda's older brother David was one of the first reasons for our friendship. I thought David was the most handsome guy in the world.

David was nineteen and I was almost thirteen. I am sure he had many laughs over my childhood crush on him. I know he was aware of it because Wanda's dad teased me about it several times. Wanda's family owned a large farm. They raised cows and strawberries and probably many things I was not aware of. Her dad also worked at the old Pevely Dairy so they always had whip cream for the strawberries. Sometimes, Wanda and I would just squirt whip cream in our mouths from the cans. I did get to spend the night occasionally there, but I don't think I did that often.

Bill and I would walk to the farm on Saturdays and help pick strawberries or whatever they had to do that day. Bill had a crush on Wanda too, although he would never admit it. I loved going to that farm and being a part of that family.

Wanda was very artistic and an excellent seamstress even at thirteen years old. She could look at a dress in a Sears catalog and make one just like it. She made our graduation dresses. They were beautiful, made of white eyelet material. She also made a beautiful blue taffeta dress for our eighth grade school dance.

These dresses were my first party dresses and I treasured them. They made me feel beautiful.

After graduation, we moved away but Wanda and I kept touch with each other for over sixty years until 2007. She quit writing to me in 2008. I was not sure why. I never saw the other kids in our graduating class again.

Wanda married and moved to Austin, Texas. She had one daughter Becky. She was divorced when Becky was small. She had a stained-glass business for many years in Austin and was quite well known. Since I started this chapter my daughter Beth did some research and found out Wanda died.

DIGRESSION:

(Wanda Ruth Turrentine Fairweather, suddenly passed from this earth much too soon. She was born on October 30, 1936, and died on April 13, 2009. She is preceded in death by both her parents, Edward Lee and Myrtle; her oldest brother, David; She was a unique spirit with a real joy for living and learning. She earned three degrees in her lifetime. The last being her true love of studio art, where she made custom stained-glass windows in the Austin area.

Austin was also the love of her heart where she lived with many people in the white hall co-op. She made many life-long friends and adored the diversity the openness of the Austin culture. She had a wonderful sense of humor and was loving and generous with friends, family and her church.)

GRADUATION: FERN RIDGE GRADE SCHOOL-1949

As I said before, Wanda had made our dresses for graduation. It was a short ceremony since there were only seven of us to graduate. We had picked our class song which was "Far Away Places." It may have been an omen because being the poorest kid in that class, I would see more "Far Away Places" than any of them. My graduation was very special to me because Mom was there. She had only met Mrs. Graham once before at Beva's graduation. We had some cookies and punch and it was over.

Jimmy Dorenias/for The Californian   2nd Row
The fifth annual commencement ceremony at Cuyamaca College Thursday afternoon was attended by 43 of the 158 eligible graduates. The college opened with 1,000 students in the fall of 1978, three months after the passage of Proposition 13. It now enrolls more than 3,000 students.

Mother, three children earn Cuyamaca degrees

I would go to college with four of my children many years later in 1981-83. I had quit high school in the second week of my sophomore year. I only had Mrs. Graham and the school of hard knocks to thank for my education. I did as well in college as my children who had all finished high school.

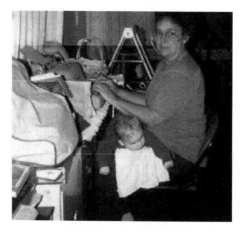

How I finished college

*Graduation, Cuyamaca College, El Cajon, CA. Gina,
left, Jo Ann, center, Beth, right.*

I even made the Dean's list one semester, as did one of my girls,
Gina. After graduating with my children, I was able to find Mrs.
Graham and thank her. She still lived in Missouri near the old
school which, of course, was gone by this time. We were able to
visit her several more times after that visit. I had the opportun-
ity to get know Mr. Graham too. They were wonderful caring
people. I am so thankful God put them in my life).

FLORIDA

Shortly after Mom and Buck were married, Buck wanted to go to Florida to look for work. Mom had a sister, Aunt Teresa in Florida. So, we packed everything into the car, gave away our dogs and drove to Florida.

Aunt Teresa was even smaller than Mom. She was only 4 feet 6 or 7. She was married to John Crites. Aunt Teresa and Uncle John had 12 children at this time. They would eventually have 16 that lived. My Uncle John Crites was a heavy equipment operator, when he worked. But the family followed the harvest from Florida picking oranges and to Washington State picking apples. All the kids that were old enough to work picked the fruit also. They traveled in an old school bus which had been converted into a bedroom or sort of motor home.

When we were there in Florida, they lived in a very little house with one bedroom and kitchen and the school bus. All the kids slept in the old school bus. We thought this was great. They all seemed very happy. My uncle john played guitar and every stringed instrument and most of the kids could play too. They sometimes made extra money playing in bars or at dances. We were so impressed and had a great time with them. I guess Uncle Buck did not find work there or changed his mind because after a few days, we returned to Missouri and the cabin in Creve Coeur Lake.

After returning from Florida, we had been able to get our little dogs Tina and Tim back.
Uncle Buck did love to fish and so did Mom. We went camping and fishing at all the lakes around Missouri. We loved it too. We were allowed to wander off and explore all the areas we camped in. We had many adventures.

OREGON

The next summer, I guess it was Uncle Buck's vacation time. He told us we were going to Oregon to look for work there. This time we had to give up one of our little dogs. There was no room in the car for two of them. We chose to give Tina up and kept Tim. This was very hard for all of us. We found some neighbors to take Tina. I guess Mom left most of her possessions with her family and we took the bare necessities with us. Buck had a 1951 Plymouth. He, Mom and Beva sat up front most of the time. The rest of us had the back seat with whatever else we had packed into the car and Timmy the dog. We camped out every night and fished when we could.

Buck would shoot rabbits for food and sometimes if there was a field of corn, other vegetables or watermelons close to the road we would help ourselves to food for the day. Sometimes, there were abandoned houses that we would stay in. Most of the time we slept outside. I refused to sleep outside even if I had to sleep across the hump on the front floorboard. I was afraid of coyotes or other animals like snakes.

Mom always managed to have flour and sugar. She made fried bread or pancakes so I don't remember ever being hungry.

It was a great trip as I recall except, somewhere along the way, Timmy got away from us. He was killed on the road by a car. That devastated us all. The people didn't even stop. Uncle Buck yelled at all of us for not watching the dog more carefully. Now I realize that he was just hurting too.

Again, we only spent about one day in Oregon and turned around and headed back to Missouri. On the trip back to Missouri, we stopped to visit an old aunt of Uncle Buck's. This was the first of his family I ever remember meeting. They had a big farm in Salina, Kansas and it was harvest time. All the farmers came and helped each other with getting the hay in the barns.

Then all the women prepared food and there was a big picnic. I remember everybody ate together after the work was done. It was a great time.

We again returned to the cabin at the lake and begged the neighbors to return our dog Tina. They reluctantly returned her to us after many tears and we told them what had happened to Timmy.

JOHNNY'S TAVERN AND STORE

There was a tavern and small store about a mile away from the Lake called Johnny's. The road to the store had a railroad track along one side. We didn't know Judy (our mule) was afraid of trains. One day, Bill rode Judy to the store and the train came by. Judy reared up and threw Bill off. She ran home alone.

After that we tried not to ride there when we knew the train might come. As it happened, one day Sally and I were coming back from the store riding Judy and we could hear the train coming. We got off and tied Judy to a fence and tried to hold her ears thinking if she couldn't hear the train she would be ok. She heard the train. She almost tore the fence down kicking and pulling on the reins. We never rode her to the store after that, at least I didn't.

It was never a good thing for Mom to go to town or to Johnny's alone because she would stop at Johnny's and someone would buy her a beer or two. Then, sometimes, we would have to go get her and bring her home from there. When this happened, there was usually a fight with Uncle Buck and he would destroy furniture, radio's etc. and leave us for a few days until he cooled off. I think he took his anger out on the things he gave us to keep from hurting mom. I only remember one physical fight with Uncle Buck and I think it escalated because my older sister Beva threw a plate at him

We lived at the lake until I graduated from Fern Ridge in 1949.

From there we moved to Kimmswick, Missouri in the fall of
1949.

* * *

CHAPTER THREE- MOVING TO KIMMSWICK, MO 1949

S hortly after graduation from Fern Ridge Elementary we were on the move again. On one of Uncle Buck's and Mom's fishing trips to the Mississippi river they found the town of Kimmswick, Missouri.

EARLY HISTORY OF KIMMSWICK:

This historic riverfront town of Kimmswick, Missouri, is nestled among tall trees and rolling hills along the Mississippi River, just 22 miles south of St. Louis. Take I-55 South to Exit 186, East to Highway 61-67, South to Highway K.

An early settler here was Captain George Washington Waters from Massachusetts. Upon graduation from the Military Academy at West Point, he was sent to Jefferson Barracks, outside of St. Louis, Missouri. Later he was appointed Jefferson County Surveyor. From this position, he was able to purchase on the courthouse steps for the sum of twenty dollars a large portion of the Labarge land grant.

It was from Captain Waters' family that Theodore Kimm purchased land on October 4th, 1850.

In 1850, a German dry goods merchant, Theodore Kimm, purchased about 160 acres of land from the widow of Captain George Waters. Kimm, a native of Brunswick, Germany, laid out the small town. He named the town he founded after himself and his birthplace by combining the words into "Kimmswick." Our definition of the word "wick" means a town or a village. The early German community was settled by wealthy families from St. Louis and immigrant stonecutters.

The town prospered early on due to easy access to railroad and river transportation. The St. Louis Iron Mountain and Southern Railroad came through in 1858 and a stream of settlers, trades- men and farmers came with it.

In those early years Kimmswick flourished with a community of 1,500 that was served by a post office, two train stations, an iron forge, iron works foundry, grist mill or flouring mill, lime- stone quarries and large greenhouses that shipped fresh flowers to St. Louis.

"The town boasted a bank, several hotels, lumber mill a lum- ber yard, brewery, saloons, mercantile stores, a slaughter house, butcher shops, a bootery, a jewelry store, a barber shop, a drug store, a blacksmith and three schools, one for whites, one for blacks. St Joseph Catholic Church and school was closed in 2007 and moved to Imperial, Missouri. This was the church where Gene and I were married in 1955; also where our son Jim and Dianna were married in 1976.

Many who settled in Kimmswick were stonemasons. They cut the limestones to build the old courthouse in St. Louis from the quarries surrounding Kimmswick. At one time, there were four- teen mineral springs in the area which were the source of salt used by the early American Indians.

Mr. Kimm laid out his town in a grid pattern of blocks subdiv- ided by lots and alleyways. He sold vacant lots and even built some houses and sold them on trust deeds to encourage many tradesmen to settle in Kimmswick. By 1876, Kimmswick was the second largest town in Jefferson County

The post office for the area was located in Kimmswick in 1858 with Mr. Kimm serving as the first postmaster. Mail arrived five times a day. Four trains going north and five trains heading south stopped each day. The historic city of Kimmswick still has a charming little post office and it is one of Kimmswick's most beloved places. A United States Post Office has been in continuous operation in the town of Kimmswick since 1858, making it one of the longest standing United States Postal Service operations in Missouri.

In 1872, Mr. Kimm retired at the age of 61. At an auction, all the unsold lots in town were offered for sale. Mr. Kimm dedicated to the inhabitants of the town an area at the corner of Third and Market Streets to be used as a public market place.

He set aside a portion of a block for a public park, Jefferson Square. It will be on your left as you enter town. He also gave an acre of ground on the western limits of his holdings for a city cemetery.

After the property sale, Mr. and Mrs. Kimm traveled to Europe, returning to St. Louis for visits. Kimm died in St. Louis in 1876 and was buried in the park, Jefferson Square, beside their only child, Ernest Peltzer-Kimm, who died at the age of nine in 1853.

Mr. Kimm continued traveling and according to one newspaper account made twenty nine crossings of the Atlantic Ocean. In a March 17th, 1886 newspaper column was this reference: "Theodore Kimm, our old and esteemed friend and the founder of our town, died in Switzerland on the 5th of February last."

OTHER ATTRACTIONS IN KIMMSWICK

In the years of the late nineteenth century there was still adequate and frequent public transportation to Kimmswick. On the north end of town was Montesano Springs Park, a large amusement park owned by the Columbia Excursion company, which attracted visitors by the thousands. Arriving by steamboats such as the "Providence" or the "J & S" and by trains, a twenty one mile ride from St. Louis, and the people came to partake of the mineral waters from the fourteen springs within the park. The water was bottled and shipped as far away as New York. In the park was a hotel and restaurant, a dance pavilion, boating lake, merry-go-round, roller coaster, pony track, bowling alleys, shooting gallery, "Herr Bismark's Tent Show" and other attractions.

John O'Heim ran a beer garden called Kimo-Garden in Kimmswick that contained a mineral spring. He bottled and sold the water under the name "Uncle John's Health Water". Tax records in 1895 show that merchant licenses were issued to the "Rising Sun Tea Company", peddler "Banana John", and to the "Kickapoo Indian Medicine Show".

Tax records also show that several showboats came to town many times through the years. "The Cotton Blossom", "Greater New York", "French's New Sensation", "Water Queen", and W.R. Marlin's "Golden Rod" were some that came frequently. The last showboat to appear at Kimmswick was the "Hollywood Showboat" on May 3rd, 1933.

The early meetings of the Town Board took place in the public school or the National Hotel. Through the years many discussions and plans arose to build a City Hall and Jail, but all came to naught.

The Town Marshall did not seem to have any problems until May 31st, 1897, when he presented a bill for a pair of handcuffs he needed. A City Hall with two Jail cells was built in 1903. Kimmswick had its own volunteer fire department until March 31st, 1940, when they paid the Arnold Fire Department for protection. The last fire truck was sold on September 29th, 1941 for one hundred dollars.

Eight new gas lights for the streets were purchased on August 10th, 1910 for six dollars each. Two brothers, Mike and Alois Ziegler, were paid to light them each evening. It wasn't until

January 3rd, 1921, that the electric street lights were installed.

The old bridge at Rock Creek was moved to Kimmswick and put in place in 1930.The Keystone Bridge Company constructed this bridge to be placed across the River des Peres at Ivory Avenue in St Louis. It remained there until 1928 when it was replaced by a new bridge and moved to Kimmswick. It is a pedestrian bridge today.

The Kimmswick Marching Band was a volunteer group and many photographs survive showing them in their smart uniforms.

The Woodman Hall at the corner of Third and Elm Streets was torn down sometime during the 1950's but many can remember the great dances held there for so many years. baseball games were the favorite sport of summer and Kimmswick's team was very active, playing all the teams from surrounding towns.

On August 27th, 1917, Kimmswick got its first speed limit on autos, eight miles per hour and fines of not less than twenty five dollars, not more than one hundred dollars. On September 9th, 1917, a reward was offered for information on the person responsible for tearing down the speed limit signs. The last hitching posts were removed from the city streets on November 4th, 1927.

As the automobile became the preferred mode of transportation and new highways were built which passed by the town, life and activities in Kimmswick changed dramatically. The river boats and passenger trains no longer stopped. Businesses moved to flank the new highways and the town was almost forgotten. The loss of boat and train traffic and the building of nearby Highway 55 almost sealed the fate of Kimmswick. Kimmswick fell into disrepair.

Many historic buildings fell into decay and were torn down,

such as the National Hotel and the Woodsmen Hall. Woodsmen Hall was revived in the 1970s and 1980s after Lucianna Gladney Ross bought several of the old buildings and leased them to shopkeepers while helping them redevelop the property.

Some of the houses that were restored included the Vaughn-Nies House in 1866, Anheuser Museum and Estate 1867, Wagner House in 1880, Wenom-Drake House in 1877, Windsor Harbor Road Bridge in 1874, Winery in 1859, and the Old Yellow House. Ross' family operated the Seven-Up Company for many years. Lucinda Gladney Ross died on Jan.24, 2012.

"Kimmswick carves out a unique niche in history. The Mississippi River town is added to the National Register of Historic Places, population in July 2007, 102, males, 46 (45.7%), females, 56 (54.3%). According to research there were no registered sex offenders living in this city in July, 2011." Signed on September 12, 2007. Robert Kelly ST. LOUIS POST-DISPATCH

Shopping ~ Dining ~ History ~ Festivals

KIMMSWICK
Missouri

Annual Events

Strawberry Festival
(First Full Weekend in June)

Girlfriends Days
(Dates listed on Website)

Witches' Night Out
(October)

Apple Butter Festival
(Last Full Weekend in October)

Christmas Open House & Parade
(Saturday before Thanksgiving)

Christmas Festival & Cookie Walk
(First Weekend in December)

For a full schedule of events: GOKimmswick.com & Facebook/GoKimmswickMO

636.464.6464
Tuesday-Friday: 10-4
Saturday & Sunday: 10-5
Closed on Mondays

Established in 1859

6000 Windsor Harbor Road
Kimmswick, MO 63053
Website
Facebook Link
Phone: 636-464-7407
TBenack@CityOfKimmswick.org
April-Nov.: Thu., noon-4 p.m.; Sat., by appointment.

The museum is in the ancestral home of Fred and Mabel Ruth Anheuser. It is located 25 miles south of downtown St. Louis. The home, built in 1867, sits at the south end of the town by the Mississippi River at Water's Point.

The Anheuser family bought the estate in 1916 and used it as a summerhouse until 1945, when Mabel-Ruth and her husband Frederick Straub Anheuser moved there. The Anheuser collection includes family heirlooms, antiques, portraits, and a family library.

Accenting the collection are Mrs. Anheuser's Westward Ho Crystal collection and a pair of 1904 hand-carved World's Fair beds. The grounds feature splendid views of the river; bald eagles are often spotted soaring above the bluffs.

Private events may be scheduled on the grounds, overlooking the Mississippi River.

Come Explore the Many Historic Sites of Kimmswick

H. Historical Society & Museum
636.464.8687
Open Weekends 1 to 4 pm.
Kimmswick's Historical Museum
with the town's history through pictures and
memorabilia. Admission is FREE. Group tours
available by reservation.

C. Burgess-Row House & Museum
Open Sundays April - October
from 1 to 4 pm. This is the first
log building to be moved to
Kimmswick (1970). Maintained and furnished by the
Kimmswick Historical Society as an 1850's
farmhouse.

WINDSOR HARBOR on RIVER

Anheuser Museum & Estate
Open Thursdays April to
November, Noon to 4 pm.
The home, built in 1867, is the ancestral home of
Fred and Mabel Ruth Anheuser and sits at the
south end of the town on the **Mississippi River** at
Water's Point. Admission $5.00. **Group tours** by
reservation. Available for weddings and events. For
information and tours, contact **Kimmswick City Hall**
at 636.464.7407.
Weekly Event: Anheuser Thursdays - Lunch at The
Blue Owl, Dessert, Beverage, plus tax & gratuity, a
Shopping Passport for participating Merchants, and a
Guided Tour of the Anheuser Estate. Call
636.464.3128 for more details or to make a
reservation.

P. Historic Post Office
In continuous operation in the City of
Kimmswick since 1858. Donated to
the City by Lucianna Gladney Ross, December 2010.

Map of Kimmswick

Lucianna Ross restores Kimmswick, MO, 1970's

In Memory of Lucianna Gladney Ross

Lucianna Gladney Ross was our
Matriarch of Kimmswick. As an
heir to the 7-Up Co., Mrs. Ross
had the monies to invest in a
project. As a child, she and her
family would travel to their
summer home in Kimmswick.
People came by train or river-
boat to enjoy time in this popular
river town. As time passed, the
highways were built making auto-
mobiles popular, and the riverboats and trains stopped
coming. The condition of the town became very
run-down. Mrs. Ross visited Kimmswick in the 1970's
and her heart was broken as historic buildings had
been torn down or were in deplorable condition. She
decided to restore and revitalize the town, this became
her project for many years to come! Mrs. Ross passed
away on January 24, 2012, at the age of 96. In 2013,
Mrs. Ross' family gifted The Visitor Center building to
the Kimmswick Historical Society. It was her desire that
the Maul House continue to serve as a welcome center
for guests. Our promise as Kimmswick Merchants is to
keep her spirit and vision alive!

Enjoy the Hospitality

of our restaurants, wide variety of
goods in our many gift shops and
galleries, or tour one of our
wonderful museums. Forty-four
buildings within the seven block
commercial district have been
recently added to The National
Registry of Historic Places.

Public Restrooms are available at
the Kimmswick Visitor Center as
well as all Dining Establishments.

**Kimmswick is located 25 minutes
south of downtown St. Louis.
Take I-55 south to exit 186**

HISTORY OF KIMMSWICK IN 1950 AS WE KNEW IT

As you come into town on K Rroad, there is a community park
on the left side of the road. The Kimms are buried there.

The main street, Market Street was about three blocks long, deserted and very quiet, dead ending at the rail road tracks and the old train station.

The first house in town, occupied now by the Wisdom family, sat on a hill across from the park. Around the first curve in the road was what had been an old, very large hotel. By 1950, it needed paint. The Edney family lived there.

Mrs. Edney's husband had died and she took care of her father who was paralyzed. I suppose he had had a stroke. She had at least six children; only three were still at home in 1950. They were my best friend Mary, her sister Carol and a brother, Gene. Another son, Jack, lived upstairs with his wife and little boy. I think Mrs. Edney took in laundry to help support her family.

Next to their house was a big vacant lot. This had been the farmers market place set aside by Mr. Kimm when he established the town.

On the next corner were the Wittu's. Mrs. Wittu was from Poland and still did not speak good English. They had five boys. Alvin and Ben lived with her. Another son Frankie, his wife Jackie, and their little boy lived in the front of the house. The oldest boy, Otto, was in the military. Mrs. Wittu's husband had drowned in the Mississippi River with one of her boys. Alvin, eighteen, worked at the shipyards in St Louis and Ben, fifteen, was still in school. Mrs. Wittu raised chickens to support herself and family.

Next to the Wittu's lived a boy named Ernie Willis and his mom. Ernie, for some reason, had a very flat head, sort of deformed. He seemed intelligent enough. The boys, of course, called him "flat-top". Ernie, my brother Bill, and Paul Weber's younger brother Butch were about the same age. These three became friends. Ernie moved away shortly after we moved in and Butch died in a car accident a few years later at age seventeen.

One of my mom's sisters and her family moved into the house that Ernie and his mom left. It was another abandoned house next to the one we moved into.

The Webers lived in the brick house on the corner. Paul Weber and my friend Mary Ida had younger sisters named Rosie and Carol who were the same age as my sister Sally, They quickly became friends. Mrs. Weber was divorced. She worked for a man named Dewey, taking care of his invalid wife. Dewey spent most weekends at the Weber's. There was some gossip in town about them.

Mrs. Weber had six children but only three lived with her. Paul, the oldest boy was seventeen, Butch, thirteen and Rosie, about ten. Norma, the oldest was a high paid call girl for the mob, the gossips said. She eventually was found dead. Several people were found dead in St Louis in the '50s in trunks of the Yellow Cab Business. Violet or "Shorty", as she was known, was married and lived in the city. Eileen, age fifteen, was adopted and lived in Chicago area with an aunt until she was sixteen. She came home the summer we moved to Kimmswick. Paul, quit school and worked at a gas service station to help his mom. Later he went in the Navy. Butch joined the navy also and was killed in a car accident when he came home on boot camp leave. Paul, who was my first boyfriend, killed himself in 2010. He called me shortly before doing this. He had COPD and his wife Jackie, had died before him. We remained friends all our lives.

All these houses were very run down, needed paint and had no inside plumbing, except for a sink in the kitchen with a hand pump for water. They did have electricity. Most had been abandoned by their owners when they died or moved away. I guess most moved to the city for work.

Down the street, on the corner of Market and 2nd there was a jewelry store owned by Mike Ziegler. The Ziegler's were one of the oldest residents and probably the most affluent family at this time, as mentioned in the history above. The Zieglers' were responsible to light the old gas lamps in 1910-1921.

In 1921, electric street lights were installed on Market Street. I think there were three lights, one on each of the three blocks. Mike was now the time keeper. He rang a bell each evening at five p.m. when he closed his store so everyone could set their clocks to the right time. He rented half of his building to a dentist who came to town one day a week.

One of Mike Ziegler's brothers lived across the street and had two teen-age girls, Carolyn and Rita Mae.

At the end of the street were the Andersons who had four boys, Red, Doug, Bruce and Little Red (David).

The corner by the jewelry store was where all the kids gathered and hung out. Sometimes they would play a game in the middle of the street called "Kick the Can". Most of the time they would just sit on the curb and hang out.

There were very few cars in town after those who worked got home so the street was safe to play and walk in. Sometimes the dogs lay down right in the middle of the street. When bored, some kids would walk out K Road about one mile and watch the traffic going to St Louis; occasionally even hitchhiking a ride to the city and back just to go someplace different.

Many people hitchhiked then, even though you could buy an old Ford for two hundred dollars and gas was only nineteen cents a gallon. Most were still too poor to afford a car.

Many times, we kids would walk to the river to sit and watch the boats and barges going to and from St Louis. We would sing songs and write poetry. Sometimes we'd go fishing or swimming in the river. I would wade in the river but never swim in it. The Mississippi River was called "Old Muddy" because it was.

The Tavern owned in 1950 by Ma and Rubin Green is now a bakery and restaurant called the Blue Owl. Those who had the price of a soda or beer would go to Ma Green's Tavern. Even if they didn't have the price of a soda, that is where everyone hung out. Someone would play the juke box and we could dance.

Rubin and Ma lived in the back of the tavern. Rubin, as well as most of the older men in town, drank a lot. He usually went to bed early and Ma would be in charge. They had two teen age grandsons, Vernon and Wayne. Their whole family spent almost every evening at the tavern. Usually every night there would be the same drunks at Green's. Harry Anderson and a couple of his teen age boys, Red and Doug. Red Anderson was not especially good looking. He had red curly hair and wore glasses, but he was one of the best dancer in town. Doug was quiet and was the kid everyone used to have run errands for them, like getting their drinks etc. I think the boys came with their dad to make sure he got home ok. Never saw Mrs. Anderson in the tavern. Hardly any of the older women went to the tavern. Some of the younger married women came with their husbands and kids. Kids were allowed in taverns with their parents because most taverns also served food.

There were several unique characters living in Kimmswick at this time. Jake Zeigler, Mike's brother, who was never married was sort of slow. After a few beers, Jake would take a salt shaker and pour salt in a pile on the bar and then balance his glass of draft beer tilted in the salt. When it was balanced, Jake would stand up for everyone to see and yell, "Ain't that a Wumpus cat!". Never knew what a Wumpus cat was. Not sure there is such a thing.

Eddie Gerard, would start for home after drinking too much. Eddie was an alcoholic, as I guess many were, but Eddie had what they called the DT's. He saw things that weren't there. I am sure the boys that teased him didn't realize how sick he was at the time. They would follow him out and yell things like "rat" or snake" just to watch Eddie go almost crazy with fear and shaking. Sad.

Another slow person was Teddy Hammmer. Teddy would walk into town on K Road usually before dark, but he had to go home in the dark after drinking too much. K Road was extremely dark after you left the last street light of town. Sometimes a few of the boys would lie in wait to scare Teddy as he went home. They thought this too was funny.

Usually, as happens, when people drink, there is generally a brawl or fight and this happened almost every night at Green's. Sometimes, one of the boys, Vernon or Ben Wittu, would like a certain song on the juke box and would play that song over and over. They would not let anyone else put money in to play a different song. This usually ended up by someone inviting Ben and Vernon outside where a fight would take place and the winner got the juke box. Sometimes an older or more sober guy would break up the fight and send them all home. Ma served beer to all who had the price if they were old enough to have a job or serve in the military. That was sixteen or seventeen years old.

THE MARKET

At the end of Market St and Front St, was one more business, a small grocery store called Julie's. Across Front St and to the left from Julie's was the train station, and across from the station was the post office.

On the outer edge of town, a place called Windsor Harbor had a marina. This was the home of a boy named Chuck Hopkins or "Hoppie". Mr Hopkins worked for the Coast Guard. Sometimes he would have to pull people who had drowned out of the river, He also repaired boats and supplied fuel to boaters and barges traveling the river.

My first experience meeting this family was shortly after moving to Kimmswick. One evening, Ben Wittu ran down the street past our house, yelling, "Floater." I had no idea what this meant. Everyone was running towards the river and I followed. When I got to the river, I saw something being pulled in by a boat. I thought it was a dead animal. I later found out it was a body of a man who had committed suicide, jumping off a bridge in St Louis. I never went to look again. It was a horrible experience. We were all thankful for Mr. Hopkins to do this job. I loved the river just to sit by it and watch it roll, to see the different boats and barges go by. It is so peaceful and soothing, but since that day I never wanted to swim in it.

Hoppie and his wife Fern now own the marina. It is a very popular spot for people all over the world who travel the river to stop or just refuel. The way I hear it, Hoppie can repair just about anything and he and Fern are great hosts.

My favorite place to spend a day is in Kimmswick at the Hopkins Marina and watch the river roll on. Kimmswick, was one of the last places we visited together before Gene died in 2011.

MOVING IN TO KIMMSWICK 1949-1950

Shortly after my graduation from Fern Ridge Elementary, we were on the move again. On one of Uncle Buck's and Mom's fishing trips to the Mississippi River they found the town of Kimmswick, Missouri. We found an old abandoned house in June of 1950 and decided to move to Kimmswick.

Bainter Children 1950
in Kimmswick, Mo

In 1949, my family of five kids, my mom and step-father moved to Kimmswick one evening just before dark. I suppose we chose that time so no one would be aware that we were moving into an abandoned house. As we began to unload the car, a teen-age boy came down the street. He was wearing his school sweater, which was the thing to do those days.

My sister Beva, who was almost seventeen, yelled at him, "Hey cutie, what school do you go to?" "Crystal", he said and continued down the street, disappearing around the corner. He was gone about five minutes and returned with several more boys.

My sister and I both thought this was great, but mom was upset with us and them. They offered to help us move in, but Mom told them no, letting them know they were not welcome. As they walked away, one of them said, "If she thinks we are bad now, wait till we get those girls out on a Saturday night."

It was many Saturday nights before we were ever allowed away from the front door after dark. As it turned out, Mom got to know these boys and all were always respectful to her and us girls.

We kids were never really aware that someone must have owned these houses we called home. I guess we thought that people got tired of living in them or they didn't want to repair them so they just moved on as we did. Maybe Beva knew but I didn't, or I was probably just preoccupied with being a teenager and never gave it a thought.

The house was a big old house which had not seen a coat of paint for many years. We went into the house and started to check it out as we had on many of our fishing trips. Inside the front door, there was a nice old staircase and hallway with a door leading to a basement under the stairs.

The basement was not finished, just a cellar probably used to keep canned goods in like a pantry. There was a large room on each side of the hall. On the left was what would become Mom and Uncle Buck's bedroom. On the right was another large room that became our living room.

A large kitchen at the back had a hand pump on the kitchen sink for water. No inside bathroom, but there was an outhouse in the back yard. Upstairs, the two rooms became the girls' and boys' bedrooms. We girls were thrilled to finally have our own room.

Bill by yellow house in Kimmswick

As we got acquainted with Kimmswick and made friends, it soon began to feel as though we had always lived there. It was home. I lived in Kimmswick only between the ages of fifteen and seventeen. For the most part, we were content. Even Mom seemed happy for a time.

That first summer changed not only my life but myself as well. I guess it was having close friends and just becoming a teenager. Some of these changes were not good. I argued more with my mom and made decisions she didn't approve of. My previous close friends did not live close by and all our activities were at their house or ours. The kids in Kimmswick were a lot less supervised.

As I said before, most of our friends were from single mom households and, even if a father was present, he was not much concerned with the kids. I am not saying we did bad things or were bad kids. We just didn't ask permission to go to the river or get a ride to the city, etc.

The mothers were too occupied with working to put food on the table and just surviving, and I think too embarrassed by their situations, to visit each other. They only spoke to each other when passing on the street.

I remember one day the local priest stopped by our house to see if he could offer us help. Mom always wore jeans and went barefoot around the house. When he came in, Mom was standing by the ice box trying to hide her feet under it so he would not see she was barefoot. She would always say to us kids, "Don't tell anyone our business." I used to wonder what "business" we had.

Mary Ida Edney and I became best friends. Mary was a very plain, skinny girl. I liked her outgoing spunk. She was a leader and at this time I was shy. I would go places and do things with Mary that I would never have done alone. I guess most of us can relate to this.

I did not know how to dance when we moved to Kimmswick. My sister Beva did and was really good, so was Mary Ida. Between them, they taught me to jitter-bug or boogie. In Missouri, it was acceptable for girls to dance together in the 50's, at least the fast dances. Mary and I got to be very good dancers. Mary, my sister Beva and I were about the only girls in town under age for drinking that were allowed to date or go to Ma Green's Tavern to dance to the juke box. All the boys went to Green's so we had plenty of dancing partners.

Even the older men that came to Green's would dance with us and taught us the waltz, polka, fox trot, shottish and other dances. There were other girls in town like the Ziegler girls but their fathers kept them close to home after dark. They didn't trust those unruly boys.

Those boys, as it turned out, respected the girls who demanded respect. I have stayed lifelong friends with all of them and their wives. I love them like my brothers. Which actually is what we became, family. It is hard for me to believe we only really knew each other for a little over two years between ages fifteen and seventeen, and yet the bonds of those teenage years became the strongest friendships of my life. I drew on those experiences most of my life to become the person I am today. We loved, we kissed, we danced, we laughed, we cried, we fought, and we grew.

Ma Green's became the center of our lives. If Mary or I found a job to do for someone like clean house, we might have enough money for a soda or two. Most of the time it was a grape soda and two straws to share. I never wanted to drink or smoke, just dance. Dancing was free and fun. Mary did smoke and drink but didn't make enough to afford her getting drunk. A soda cost only a nickel those days. I think beer was a quarter. After I learned to dance, that was all I wanted to do.

Carol, *Beva and Phyllis Vittoe in Kimmswick, Mo.*

Shortly after we moved in and got settled, another family moved into town, the Grimshaws. They had twelve children. Two of the older girls, Dee Dee and Georgia, became good friends with Beva and me. They were both really good dancers as were their two brothers Donnie and Jerry. Beva had a mad crush on Donnie. He was very good looking. It was a great summer.

Grimshaws and Kimmswick Kids

At sixteen, I got a job at a local restaurant as a dish washer. It didn't pay very well only twenty-five dollars a week. When I got my first paycheck I paid Ma Green the 50 cents I owed. That was establishing credit then.

Beva got a job helping Mrs. Anhuasher clean house. She liked it and Mrs. Anhausher gave her clothes she didn't want. Beva had never had such nice clothes before.

I met the boy next door, Paul Weber. Paul asked me to go steady, and I said yes. He gave me his ring which had the head of an Indian on it and was much too big for my finger, so I wore it on a chain around my neck. I found out that Paul was jealous when I wanted to dance with the other guys, so we soon broke up. After giving Paul back his ring, I never wanted to go steady again. That way I could dance with who ever asked me.

One evening, some of the older boys decided to pick on my brother Bill. I jumped into the fight, not that I was much help. They just held their arms around me while I kicked and screamed at them. A boy I had not met before came to our aid. He was Gene Antoine and would be the boy I married.

Gene Antoine had lived in Kimmswick from age nine to sixteen. All the guys were his buddies. He had moved away from Kimmswick just before we moved in. His mom, Lula, and Ma Green's daughter, Eunice were best friends. Gene and Ma Green's grandsons, Wayne and Vernon, were raised like brothers. Gene came to town almost every weekend and we became good friends. He was one of the best dancers and I loved dancing with him.

Gene was more interested in Paul Weber's sister Eileen at this time. She had come home to live with her mom after being raised by an aunt in Chicago. Eileen was really cute we too became very good friends.

The new school year started but we didn't go to Crystal High School with that boy on the street, Donnie Allen. We were enrolled in Herculaneum High. Everyone referred to it as Herky. The kids from Crystal City jeered at us at the football games, "Herky's Jerky" so they became our arch rivals in sports.

Jo Ann on Publications Committee. Herculaneum High School. 1951

It was all so new to me, riding a school bus, changing rooms for different teachers and subjects. I really liked high school and did well that first year.

On my sixteenth birthday, August 20th, 1951, Gene, Paul and Alvin all joined the Navy together and left Kimmswick.

Alvin was dating Dee Dee Grimshaw. Most of the girls really liked Alvin Wittu. He was not a great dancer but was always the life of the party. Joking and making everyone laugh.

Gene was dating Eileen Weber, Paul had met a girl from St Louis, Maxine. Max and I had become good friends.

I was dating Roy Moyers, a new boy from St. Louis. Roy joined the Navy and was in boot camp with these guys. Even though Gene did not know Roy before, Gene and Roy were bunk mates and became friends when they realized they both knew me.

Circulation 3350   Hillsboro, Misso

TWO KIMMSWICK BOYS ENLIST IN NAVY

(Left to right) Paul Weber, 17, son of Mrs. Reba Mae Weber, Kimmswick, Mo., Eugene Antoine, 17, son of Mr. and Mrs. Arthur Weber, 4715 N. 20th Street, St. Louis, Mo., and Alvin Wittu, 19, son of Mrs. Albina Wittu, Kimmswick, Mo., were sworn into the Navy on Aug. 20, by Lieut. Cmdr. H. C. Teaford, officer in charge, U. S. Navy Recruiting Station, St. Louis, as Paul Sibley of Kimmswick, Mo., looks on.

Sibley is the sponsor of the Kimmswick Athletic Club of which Wittu is the president and Antoine is the vice-president.

The men left Lambert Field, St. Louis, Missouri, Monday, Aug. 20, at 9:15 p.m. CST, and arrived in San Diego, California at 10:40 a.m. Tuesday, Aug. 21. They will be stationed at the Naval Training Center, San Diego, California for recruit training.

Paul Weber, Eugene Antoine, Alvin Wittu. Enlistment

(Left to right) Paul Weber, Jo Ann and Gene Antoine, Visiting in 1979

I started my second year of high school. Alvin came home on his boot camp leave. He came to the high school and Mary and I skipped classes and left the school grounds with him. We got caught when we returned to the school to get the bus home. We were called into the office by one of the teachers, Mrs. Robinson. She told us how disappointed she was in our behavior, especially mine, because she had done everything she could to help me stay in school. I was embarrassed to know that anyone had to help me, so, very flippantly, I told her I didn't need or want her help and I was quitting school right then. She said I had to ride the bus home because the school was responsible until I got home.

THE RUN AWAYS...AGAIN

I have lived to regret many times in my life being that smart-alecky teenager with an attitude. This was a time of change for me that I did not handle very well. I don't know if I told my mom that day I quit school or if I just started trying to find a job and be on my own.

At any rate, my mom and I got into an argument about my staying out too late. She threatened to send me to live with my father, who, of course, I knew did not want me to begin with. I told her, Fine with me. I am going", and started to pack what little I owned. This had never happened before when she threatened us. We always apologized and shut up. But this time I decided I would leave.

The first thing I started to pack was my graduation party dress Wanda, my friend from eighth grade had made for me. Mom got so angry at me, she grabbed the dress and began to rip it apart. At that moment, I hated her. Years later I would understand her anger and the sense of loss she was feeling.

I was growing up and, right or wrong, I was going to make decisions for myself. The fight stopped as I sat in the floor, holding my dress and crying, but the anger I felt for her did not stop.

The next day we didn't talk. She and Buck went into town and I made my plans. I was running away. I was too scared to go alone so I begged my friend Mary to go with me. We would get jobs in the city and get an apartment. I convinced her that we were sixteen and could go to work.

Mary and I set off for the city, hitchhiking. It was not the first time Mary and I had hitchhiked so it was not a scary thing for us. We walked out K Road and, soon enough, someone stopped and asked if we needed a lift. It was a truck driver. I think when he realized we were run aways, he had second thoughts, so he told us he could not take us into the city but would get us close to a bus line.

Joann, Lorraine and Mary Ida

Mary and I climbed down from the truck and sat on the bench at the bus stop, trying to figure out what we would do next. We had no money or a place to stay that night. The reality of what we had done was beginning to set in. Mary wanted to go back home. We could just turn around now and go back home. I knew I would be punished and did not want to face my mom again. She would probably contact my dad and ask him to take me. I really did not know him and knew he had not wanted us in the first place. He most likely would say no. As we waited and talked, I could tell Mary was wanting to go home but would go on with me if I asked.

We did have one friend Nancy Moore who lived in the city. Nancy's grandmother lived across the street from Mary's family in Kimmswick. The Moore's spent a lot of time in Kimmswick visiting their grandparents. We had not totally made up our minds to go on, when a car with an older man pulled up to the curb. He asked if we wanted a ride to save our bus money, which of course we didn't have. We asked if he was going to North St. Louis off Grand Ave and he said yes so, we got into the front seat, me being in the middle and Mary by the door. He asked where we lived and we told him Kimmswick then realizing that was a mistake, we made up a lie about going to visit an aunt and our mom being sick.

I got the feeling he knew it was all a lie since lying was not something I usually did. I mostly tried always to evade the truth rather than out and out lie. Being a Catholic we went to confession weekly or at least monthly as we became teenagers. He then asked if we would want to go out with him while we were in the city. We both answered at once that our aunt was very strict and would not let us date. I am not sure what age this man was but he was too old for either of us to consider dating. He then pulled over to the curb, gave us fifty cents, and told us that was as far as he was going. Mary already had the door open and I was hurrying out right behind her. As I got to the door, I felt him touch my butt. If he had raped me I would have not felt any more violated. I was really scared after this incident. All we wanted now was to get to a safe place and be with people we knew.

We went into a store and agreed Mary should buy a pack of cigarettes with her share of the fifty cents and we would each get a candy bar. We asked directions and finally found our way to the Moore's house. It was around supper time and they were just sitting down to eat. They asked if we wanted to eat but we politely said no, as we were always taught to use good manners. We were immediately sorry for that. The food smelled so good and we were both so hungry. After dinner, Nancy took us to a local tavern where the kids she knew hung out. It was just the corner bar and served sodas. Most of the kids that worked and had money could buy a beer. No one carded you those days.

We danced to the juke box and met several of the gang that hung out there. We finally told some of them that we were running away. One of the boys named Ray offered us his apartment to stay at for the night. We decided we would take his offer and go on to Illinois the next day. Why Illinois? It was the next state to Missouri.

We had gone there on occasion to some club near Scott AFB. We had met some Airmen stationed there and thought we might get a job on the base. Mary, of course, had a beer and after a couple of drinks she started feeling bad about her mom worrying about us. Her older sister, Evelyn, was living in the city. She called her and told her where we were. I was unaware of this until Evelyn showed up to take us home.

Another boy at the bar was Roy Moyers who, later, became Gene's bunk mate in the Navy. I had been dancing with him. He was really a handsome guy around eighteen. He told me that Ray was not someone we should go home with and I should just go home. I knew he was right but I was so determined to be my own boss I was not going home. When Mary decided to go with her sister, I felt I had to leave now and go on alone. I started to leave with everyone telling me not to go on alone. Then Evelyn said she was calling the police and telling them where I was. This scared me and I started to run away from all of them. I was so scared now and didn't know what to do so I just ran into the night. Roy ran after me and caught me and brought me back to the bar, telling me how dumb I was.

The police showed up and talked to Evelyn, who, I am sure, gave them the money needed to get us a bus ticket home. The police took us to the Greyhound bus station and told us they would wait there until we boarded the bus for home. We took the bus and I knew this was not the way I would ever leave home again. I was terrified at what was waiting for me at home too.

For some reason, we didn't go straight home. I think we were kind of scared to walk on K Road at that time of night. It was near eleven p.m. K Road was the darkest and almost scariest road at night. We decided to get off the bus at the local truck stop and see if we could get a ride with someone going into Kimmswick.

Almost everyone went to the truck stop for late night snacks or stopped there on their way home. We went into the restaurant and sat down. We told the waitress what we were doing. She came back with a man we didn't know. He told us he was a sheriff's deputy who had been looking for us. He would drive us home. He wasn't in uniform so, after the owner of the truck stop verified he was a deputy, we went with him. He dropped Mary at her house and when he pulled up in front of my house I was as scared as I have ever been to go into that house.

Mom opened the door and let me in. The angry look she gave me told me I was in big trouble. She said she wanted to talk to me so I sat down, trying not to look at her. She told me that what I had done would not be without some punishment. First, I was not going to Green's Tavern or anywhere by myself until she could be sure I could be trusted. I said I was sixteen and old enough to take care of myself. She slapped me across my face, which I now understand how frustrated and worried she was. She told me to go to bed. I climbed the stairs very defeated and confused as to how I would ever be able to care for myself. It was one of the most miserable times of my life.

Mom never mentioned again sending me away to my dad's after that. When I asked to do anything, or go with my friends, she would never say no. She would just say I would rather you didn't go there or do that.

I guess we both changed some after that and learned to respect her more and loved her again for letting me come home.

Home isn't just a house you live in. it is being with people you know will always love you no matter how badly you behave.

* * *

CHAPTER FOUR- LEAVING KIMMSWICK 1951-52

I guess Mom had decided she had done all she could to raise Beva, Bill and me. She could not check on where we went or who we went with. She had no phone and didn't drive. She still had Sally and David to raise. So, she let us make our own decisions.

About the only rule we had was, if we were staying the night with a friend, we must let her know. If we were coming home, we had to be in by ten p.m. on weekdays and twelve p.m. on weekends.

Before Mary Ida and I had jobs and finally left home, we were still finding rides to St. Louis to go to dances. Don't know how we heard about a place called the "Hucklebuck." It was another corner bar that had a live band. It was in a basement of an old school building. It was also where a lot of the airmen from Scott Air Force Base went.

Mary was eighteen and it was OK for her but I had just turned seventeen. The bouncers at the Hucklebuck knew I as under age but let us in. They told us if we saw the cops come in to check things out, we were to leave by the back door. This never happened. The Hucklebuck was a popular song and dance in the early '50's.

Mary and I were a sight to see. We had started to dress alike at times. The styles were beginning to change from the poodle skirts and crinolines to the tight midi skirts and turtle neck sweaters with bobby sox's and Penny-loafers" with taps. You always put a dime in the slits of the penny-loafers for mad money to call home if you needed to and if home had a phone.

Mary and I had one outfit alike, a black midi-skirt almost to the ankles and a yellow turtle neck sweater. We would bop down the streets, singing and tapping to "I've got rhythm". We thought we were as good as Gene Kelly or any of those movie stars. I am so glad they didn't have "selfies" then and this picture is only in my memory.

One evening at the "Hucklebuck", Mary met a very handsome airman named Roy. He had a beautiful red convertible. They were both drinking and Roy asked her to marry him. At this time, Missouri required a blood test that required a three day waiting period. People who didn't want to wait could go to Kentucky, Arkansas or Mississippi, all of which didn't have those laws.

I never drank, so I knew this was not a good thing and I didn't want to go with them. I told Roy that Mary and I would stay at a hotel in the city for the night and if they both felt the same way in the morning I would go with them. Thank God, they agreed. Roy drove us to a hotel, probably where airmen took girls they met. It was not in the best part of town.

Mary and I had never stayed in a hotel before. As we got out of the car, two policemen came walking their beat. They looked at us, two girls and an airman in uniform, but just walked on by. Roy waited outside while Mary and I went to see if we could get a room. The desk clerk had us sign the register. I didn't want my name on the register so Mary and I decided to use a couple of names of girls we went to school with, Barbara Abernathy and Helen McCain.

Suddenly, those two policemen entered the hotel from another entrance. Roy could see them but he didn't leave. They started to ask us questions like, "Do you live in the city?" "Why are you staying in the hotel?" Finally, "How old are you?"

I was beginning to panic. One policeman took Mary aside and the other began just to question me. I guess they separated us to see if we would give the same answers. I knew I had to be eighteen so I told him I was eighteen. The cop questioning me asked me again, "How old are you?" and what year I was born. Being very smart and knowing I had to change my birth year, I told him I was eighteen born in 1936. He asked me did we work for the hotel. I thought he meant as a maid. I had never heard the word prostitute before this. I told him, "No, we don't work for the hotel." He asked me again my age and year I was born. I knew I was lying and thought, "He's trying to trick me." So, I stuck to my story. "I am eighteen and born in 1936." By now I was getting scared and starting to cry. Finally, the other cop came over and said, "She doesn't know what you are talking about working for the hotel." Then he said to me "Young lady, you cannot be eighteen and born in 1936." "Oh No!" I realized I went the wrong way with my math. Now I was in tears. We told them it was too late to go home. There was no bus to Kimmswick till morning. They told us we could spend the night and they were on duty all night. But if we so much as opened the door to our room, we would be in trouble. They then went outside and told Roy to leave, which he did. About every two hours, the bell boy would knock on our door and tell us the cops were still out there.

The next morning Roy was back. Mary told him she wanted to get to know him better. He drove us home to Kimmswick. They dated for a while but never married. I never lied about my age again. Evidently, I was not that great at math.

THE DIRT ROAD- LEAVING KIMMSWICK AND GROWING UP- 1951-1952

Mary and I started out for the city again, but this time it was to find a real job so we could be on our own.

Sixteen going on Seventeen is a magic age as we remember in the "Sound of Music." No fear of life and every decision is exciting and new to you, because you are getting to make your own choices. Of course, you are not prepared for when those choices don't work out as you plan.

I am not sure who we hitched a ride with to the city, but we made it to downtown. We started walking from one business to the next, filling out employment forms. No one seemed interested. Finally, one of the department stores that was hiring for the Christmas season hired the two of us. We worked in different departments. My job was to sell umbrellas and hand out gift wrap boxes to the customers. Not very exciting until the first payday. It was boring and I didn't see a future of being able to leave home on that pay. I think it was $1.25 an hour. This was minimum wage at that time. We worked until after the Christmas season there but, towards the end, Mary and I missed a few days when we found something to do in town besides going to work.

We had been able to get a ride to the city with the Grimshaws. They owned a carpet cleaning business in the city so they came in every day. The older Grimshaw kids also had jobs they had gotten before they moved to Kimmswick. We all had to sit on the floor of the van because it was used to haul carpets; not people. There were no seats, but the price was right. It cost us nothing to get there. From the carpet shop we could ride public transportation. The buses and streetcars were very affordable and reliable.

One of the Grimshaw girls, Georgia, worked at a company called Brown Shoe Company. It was one of the largest companies in St. Louis at that time. They even advertised on the radio. I still remember the trademark and ad. The Trademark was a little boy and his dog. The boy said, "I'm Buster Brown. I live in a shoe. That's my dog Tide. He lives there too."

I think Georgia had already helped my sister Beva get a job at Brown Shoe Company. I was very bored with the job at the department store, so I put in my application in at the Brown Shoe Company and was hired.

Mary had already quit the department store too. Not sure where she worked after that.

My new job was a mail clerk. Each morning I opened the incoming mail. We had a machine that you put the envelopes in and it sliced them open. I then delivered the orders for shoes to each department men, women and children and the complaint department. I picked up the outgoing mail from each department and ran them through a stamp machine that stamped each one and then tied them into small bundles. We actually had a machine that tied the bundles too. This job was a step up in pay and was full time. Full time did not give you benefits then. I liked it a lot I worked there for over six months and still lived in Kimmswick.

Another of the Grimshaw girls, Gracie, was working at the Bell Telephone Company. Beva put in her application and got hired as a long-distance operator. They made more money but had to work nights and week-ends. I decided Beva and I could get an apartment in the city if I made more money, so I went to Bell and applied for a job. No one called me, so I went back to their personnel office to ask why. The lady there, Mrs. Carter, said because I had quit high school she was sure I would quit this job too.

I begged her to give me a chance and she agreed, stating I probably would not pass the testing they did. I passed and she gave me my first chance at a good company with a future. After taking my training, I got tired of having to work split shifts and nights. Split shifts worked four hours in the morning and four hours in the evening. I felt I had no life but work and all my friends were out dancing and having a good time.

Beva and I both quit Bell Telephone, a decision we both regretted later. At least I did. I never again had a job with any benefits, so I really regretted that decision a lot. Beva later worked for the post office so had a good retirement benefit, even though she lived only a couple of years after she retired.

From the telephone company, I went to work just up the street at a dress factory. I had been a mail and file clerk. Now I was in a switchboard operator, receptionist position. At least I was getting qualified for many job skills. I also got a discount on dresses through the company. First time I had a wardrobe that was decent. One day my boss was on an important call and I accidentally disconnected him. He flew into a rage, cussing me out, so I decided right then to quit that job. First, I called in sick for a couple of days and when payday came, I went in and picked up my check and quit.

I walked across the street to a little café to eat lunch and asked for a job. They hired me. I was back to $1.25 an hour and knew I couldn't make rent and car fare on that. So, after one day of filling little cups with jelly, I decided this was not for me.

My friend Maxine, Paul Weber's new girlfriend, got me a job with her at United Van Lines and I went to live with her family. My job was a mail clerk again and general office clerk. I also was trained to operate the addressograph machine as well as relief PBX switch board operator. At least I could use all the job skills I was learning.

I loved living at Max's with her family. Max had her own car so I didn't have to take the bus this was great.

Paul was away in the Navy, so we could go to all the places our friends hung out and danced. It was wonderful. One of the places the kids from Kimmswick hung out was a bar and dance hall in Herculaneum called Artisan Park. After going to the dances on weekends there, I asked for and got a weekend job waiting tables. The boss was great and said I could dance while I worked just let someone else cover my section when I danced. Great job! I danced more than I worked. The sax player and leader of the band was the best. He was on the level of Boots Randolph. This place was really a great place if you liked to dance and then to get in free and get paid for it to was to die for. Life was good at this point and fun. I dated whomever I wanted to, no steady boyfriend. Roy and I had already broken up after his first leave home. My life and decisions were all my own again.

I saw Beva and Mary when they came to Artisian on most weekends. Not sure where Beva was living at this time, probably back in Kimmswick with our family or with Mary's family.

One winter evening, after leaving Artesian we were in a car with a friend, Arland Kelso. We were going back to the city. Maxine wasn't driving because she had been in a bad accident before this and had broken her back. I think she was afraid to drive yet. Anyway, our friends, Alvin, who was home on leave from the navy, Max and her boyfriend Bob (MAX had broken up with Paul at this time), Beva and her new boyfriend, Everett Jones and I were going to party some more. Beva and Everett had just gotten engaged. Beva started to complain of a headache and, unknown to us in the front seat, each of the kids in the back seat had started to pass out from carbon monoxide.

Arland and Alvin had their vent windows opened so the windows didn't fog up and I guess this was why they didn't pass out too. They said I put my foot on the gas, and was unresponsive. They pulled off the road and started removing all of us from the car. I came to right away but was confused at what was happening. It was cold, snow on the ground. I am sure people passing by just saw teenagers and figured we were all drunk so no one stopped to help. Thank God Alvin had been trained in the navy and gave them CPR until finally the police and an ambulance and news reporters showed up. We spent the rest of the evening in the emergency room. All lived and had no ill effects. Afterwards we learned Arland had put new tail pipes on his car but hadn't installed them properly. We were all very lucky that night to survive. We made the papers again, our fifteen minutes of fame.

I was not seeing much of my family at this time. Mom, Buck, Sally and David had moved from Kimmswick across the river to Venice, Illinois to another abandoned cabin on the river there.

Bill had left home and was working in the city. He had gone to live with Gene Antoine's family because Gene's younger brother Jerry and Bill had become close friends.

One morning Mr. Brimble, Max's dad was reading the paper and said my family had all been exposed to rabies. They had a dog that had had a litter of puppies and they all had rabies. I couldn't call, as, they had no phone so I took the bus and found my way to the cabin. They were all ok but still had to take the shots, which were very painful.

I returned to Maxine's.

One weekend, Beva and Mary were hitch hiking to Kimmswick, planning to go to Artesian. They got a ride with two Marines home on leave. They made a date with them for the next evening. The very next day, as fate would have it, Mary's brother Robert who was also a Marine, was coming home on leave and hitchhiking the same highway. The same two Marines picked him up and they were all surprised that they were going to the same place. Robert was invited to come along to Artesian with them. I was working and, towards closing time, Beva came up to me and asked if I would go home with Mary and the two Marines. She wanted to be with Robert. I said ok and rode home with them. They dropped us off, not making any further dates, which I was happy about. I never saw them again. The Marine I was with was wearing a Miraculous Medal ring. I said I liked it and he gave it to me. I wore that ring out and have worn a ring like it ever since. I think it has kept me out of a lot of trouble, just seeing it on my finger.

Deputy Robert Edney (3rd from left), Kimmswick, MO.

A short time after all this, Buck and Mom decided to go to California. Beva wanted to be near Robert so she wanted to go with them. Robert was stationed at Camp Pendleton. Beva and Robert had become a couple since that night at Artesian. Bill wanted to go because he had a job at a perfume plant he didn't like. I chose to stay in Missouri. I had a good place to live and a job I liked.

I felt it was time to be on my own. I also expected they would get tired of California and come back to Missouri after a short stay, as they had always done in the past. They left and I was entirely on my own now.

I was seventeen years old then.

The year was 1952.

* * *

CHAPTER FIVE- MOVING TO CALIFORNIA 1952-53

CALIFORNIA HERE I COME

This was to become another of our travel songs; " California Here I Come", "Vagabond Shoes", "Side by Side", "The Bo Weevil Song", "Just lookin' for a home" (Beva's favorite). These were our favorite songs of that time.

BILL & BUCK 1953

My family made it to California and found a place to rent with my step-father. This was a first. Up to this time, we had always found abandoned houses. It was a very small house, only one bedroom, on Slauson Avenue in an industrial area.

Some of you probably have driven close to that area in Los Angeles. If not, it was not an area you would want to be in after dark even today.

Beva and Robert were married right away and moved to Camp Pendelton to base housing. Things seemed to be OK for them as far as I knew. I was happy back in Missouri working at United Van Lines and living with my adopted family.

That didn't last long. In about six months or so, I heard from my mom. She and Uncle Buck had split up. Uncle Buck came back to Missouri but this time Mom did not come with him.

Beva was already expecting her first baby and they weren't financially able to help Mom and the other kids.

Beva

Mom and Bill had found jobs in a parachute packing company. They got paid by how many parachutes they could pack in a day. Mom was not well physically. She had not been healthy since David was born. She worked shifts and that meant leaving Sally and David unsupervised much of the time. They were not making much money but were surviving.

I felt sorry for them and knew I could help if I was there. I decided to quit my job and move to Los Angeles. When I told Maxine and her family what I planned to do, Max's dad said he would like to go to California for his vacation. It was decided that he and Maxine would both take their vacations and drive me to California.

Another friend of ours, Phyllis Vititoe had gotten involved with a married man in Kimmswick and wanted to move away also. We all shared the cost of the trip and headed off to California. This was the first trip I remember that I actually stayed in a hotel. It was great.

When Maxine's father, Mr. Brimble, would go to his room, we three girls would leave the hotel and look for guys or places to dance. God is good to look after the stupid. We did meet boys in Texahoma, that took us dancing and were very nice guys. Not sure if Mr. Brimble ever figured out why Maxine was too tired to help him drive.

We finally got to Los Angeles and found the place my family was living. It was right on the outskirts of an area called Watts.

Watts was an all-black area of Los Angeles at that time. Later, it would become the center of racial riots. But then all was quiet and people of black, white, or Mexican decent lived in the area lived in peace. All were equally poor and just went about the business of staying alive.

Maxine and her dad just dropped Phyllis and me off, said their goodbyes, and went on with their vacation. We kept in touch but I saw Maxine only one more time after that.

Bill had managed to buy an old '35 Ford. The only thing wrong with it was the battery died every night. We would have to push it out in the street and hope someone would give him a push to get it started. These old cars would start if you bypassed the battery and got them going 20 or so miles an hour. It was more trouble than it was worth but he was a proud owner of his first car.

Bill with 1935 Ford

After about two weeks of hunting for a job in Los Angeles, I was getting very discouraged. Phyllis was getting homesick. I have never known anyone who actually got physically sick from this, but she was physically sick. She hadn't found a job either. I finally got a call from the Citizens National Bank in Los Angeles. I was hired to work as a clerk in the trust department. I worked inside the trust vault where all the wills and trusts were kept. The bank was the trustee for people's estates. It was a very interesting job. We had many wills of movie stars and very wealthy people. They also stored their jewelry in the vaults too. The bank officers were all lawyers who settled the estates when someone died.

My job was to file all the papers in the right files and sometimes, if I recognized a famous name, I would read their wills. The morning would start with reading the obituaries, checking to see if we had the wills or trusts of any of the deceased. If we had them, I would pull all the files for the trust officers when they had confirmed it was our client. I would then have to go to the Los Angeles Court House, probate department, and file all the paperwork needed to settle the estate.

I especially liked this part of the job because, when I left the bank, I either walked to the court house or took the streetcar. It was a nice break and outside.

The bank was on 3rd Street and Spring Street, I think. It was right downtown so on lunch hour I could shop the department stores if I had money, or not. Mostly we young girls would go to the record stores and listen to all the new records that were out.

Record stores in the '50's had little enclosed sound-proof booths. Customers picked out the record they wanted to listen to before they bought it. Of course, listeners were expected to buy the records, but we purchased very few of them. We just wanted to learn the words.

Four girls worked in the vault. Margaret, our boss who was a young Navy wife, probably about twenty-five; Mary Lou, nineteen; Betty, nineteen; and myself, seventeen. All had the same jobs. Mary Lou and I became life-long friends. In fact, she and her husband later were God parents for our daughter Gina.

Mary Lou came from a strict Catholic family and I would sometimes go home with her and spend the night. After working together about six months, Mary Lou decided she was tired of running around to the dances and meeting different guys. She announced to me one morning that she was going to marry the first Catholic boy she met.

We were going to a dance hall called Spade Cooley's on the Santa Monica Pier. One Saturday night when I didn't go to the dance with her, she met a very nice guy named Al Woods. Al had a friend named Frank. They were both Marines, stationed at Camp Pendleton.

The first Sunday after Mary Lou met Al and his buddy Frank, both guys showed up for church. They came every Sunday to go to church with us. After dating a short time, Frank and Al were being discharged and going home. Al was from St Louis and Frank from New York. Al and Mary Lou had decided to get married after his trip home to see his family.

One morning at work, Mary Lou was sick. She told me she

thought she was pregnant. I was shocked, since marrying a Catholic had meant so much to her. She was worried about telling her dad but also about telling Al, who had not returned yet.

I went with her to the doctor appointment to be sure she was pregnant, before she called Al to tell him. She didn't want her family to know so we went to a doctor close to work. I felt really uncomfortable. The office was sort of dark and, in my mind, what you would see in a bad movie. The doctor confirmed her worst fears and she began to worry whether Al would come back.

When she called him, he assured her he was coming back as soon as possible, but he had to tell her he was not a Catholic. He had never told her he was, but because he had been going to church with Frank, who was Catholic, Al continued to go with us. Thank God, he did return and they were married before she ever had to confront her family.

Al later became a Catholic. It was a marriage made in Heaven. They have been married for over 60 years. They had the baby, Jack and two more boys. They lived next door to her sister and her seven boys in West Los Angeles until 1976 and now live in Henderson, Nevada.

I visited with them over the years when I had the chance. But I haven't been in touch for some time now. Mary Lou wasn't feeling well and my life got pretty busy too.

After a few paychecks, Phyllis and I found a better place for all of us to live in a town called South Gate, California. It was one of the nicest places we had lived up to this time. Had inside plumbing, and we even paid rent.

Bill and Mom lost their jobs. They got laid off shortly after moving to South Gate. Phyllis told me, she had to go home because she was getting sicker. She left and now I couldn't afford the apartment. I started looking for another place to live.

Beva and Robert had their baby, a little girl. She was born premature, weighing only three pounds. So tiny, I never expected her to live, but she was a fighter and survivor. They named her Donna Marie. Donna is about 66 years old at this writing.

Bill tried to get another job and finally, with my urging and Roberts influence, he joined the marines too and left for boot camp. He could help Mom out by sending her an allotment.

Mom, Sally, David and I moved into a small one bedroom trailer in a crummy little trailer court, no bath. We had to go to the wash room to shower, a step back.

Sally babysat when she could for extra money. Mom started to babysit two little girls Linda, four and Patty, three, but their mother didn't pay mom half the time and sometimes didn't even show up to take the girls home. Mom felt sorry for them and continued to babysit them.

Bill finished Boot Camp and came home on leave. I remember sitting up all night talking and laughing at all he had to go through. He was a Marine and all grown up. Life was going ok except we needed a better place to live. This rundown, shoddy trailer was far too small and uncomfortable.

Bill had an allotment set up for Mom. It wasn't much but was a big help so we could move.

BILL 1954

We found another decent apartment not too far from the trailer park. Mom could continue to watch the girls. This apartment was a lot farther from my work but was cheaper and a better place to live. I now had to ride a bus to what they called a PE train, then walk a few blocks from the station to work. This took me over an hour each way.

On most weekends, Bill and his buddy Marines and Beva and Robert would all come home; also, Alvin Wittu from Kimms-wick and a buddy or two Navy guys. It was wall to wall people, all sleeping wherever they could on the floor.

As I look back now, I guess we were the talk of the neighborhood. Mom being a single mom, me, dating age and Sailors and Marines coming and going all hours of the night. Mom had begun dating a guy named Cliff. It was all perfectly innocent but must have looked different to the neighbors.

Alvin had introduced me to his girlfriend Janice and her twin sister, Joyce.

Joyce and I had become fast friends and would remain friends for the rest of our lives, more than 60 years or more now. She lives in North Carolina. When I wasn't spending time with Mary Lou, I was with Janice and Joyce.

The time I spent with Mary Lou became less after she and Al got married and had their baby.

Alvin, David, Joann & Gene - 1953

Joyce and Janice and I went to all the dances and there were many dance halls in Los Angeles in the '50's. We especially liked going to a tv show and dance hall called "Town Hall Party." Some of you may have watched it on tv. All the stars from the Grand Ole Opry entertained there. The dances usually had a cover charge of only a dollar or so. Everyone could afford the dances. There were at least four that had top name entertainers. Spade Cooley was an old-time film star and had guest stars appearing there. Hank Williams, Hank Snow, Brenda Lee, and others all came to Town Hall Party. It was televised only in California, I think. Tex Williams had a dance hall. He wrote the song "Smoke That Cigarette." I am sure some of you have heard it. If you loved to dance as we did, the '50's were the greatest time to be in California. We were the prelude to Dick Clark and his American Bandstand which started in the late '50's early '60's.

We also had a favorite hangout where a lot of the sailors went called the Western Corral in Long Beach. Our lives were full of work, fun, guys, and dancing. It was all perfectly safe in those days for girls to go to a dance alone. I don't know if it was because TV hadn't ruined all the morals of society or people were just more decent then. I can honestly say I met many Sailors, Marines and ordinary guys and never felt they had anything but respect for me. Like me, they just loved to dance and have a good time. It also could have been that I never drank, smoked or cussed in front of a guy. Maybe that got me the respect they gave me.

I fell in and out love with each Sailor that came home and forgot the one that just left that year.

Jo Ann 1954

As fate would have it, Joyce fell in love too but for real with Ricky (Ivan Ryan.) They were married and have stayed so for over sixty years at this writing. Joyce decided she and Ricky would go to Yuma, Arizona one weekend and get married. Not sure if she told her mom or not. Her parents didn't come with us to the wedding. Joyce's older sister, her twin, myself and some of Ricky's buddies all took off for Yuma from Compton, California.

The guys were all drinking and halfway to Yuma, we stopped to eat. Ricky got very sick from being drunk, or the heat or nerves, not sure which. I was sure Joyce should not go through with this wedding. But by the time we got to Yuma, Ricky was sober and remembered his dad had an old friend in Yuma. He called and the lady told us all to come right to her house and she would have the wedding there. What was going to be a quickie wedding at some wedding chapel turned out to be beautiful.

This lady got a minister to come, invited her neighbors and even had a piano or organ and she played the Wedding March. She even had a reception for them.

Shortly after they were married, Alvin's ship came back to Long Beach. Ricky had bought an old Model-A Ford and fixed it up. One weekend, he and Alvin, both had been drinking and they decided to go for a ride. They totaled the car on Signal Hill in Long Beach. Both went to the hospital. Ricky had really messed up his face. Not sure what other injuries he had. We thought he was going to die. Alvin escaped being hurt too bad. Joyce was already pregnant with their first baby or she might have considered leaving then. I know I would have. I remember once she told me Ricky was the only guy she knew who could get drunk on a quarter because he was so much fun everyone would buy his drinks. Drinks cost only a quarter then.

About this time, Gene Antoine from Kimmswick, had gotten discharged from the Navy and came to live in Riverside with his best friend's family. Gene and I had been writing throughout his time in the Navy. He knew my family and I had moved to California. One day he decided to look us up. He drove to Bell Gardens and realized he had left the address at John's. He stopped at a phone booth to call John but a Marine was using the phone.

He waited and the Marine kept looking at him. He, being a sailor, was sure this was going to end up in a fight. The marine stepped out of the phone booth and said to him, "Are you Gene Antoine." The marine was my brother Bill! He had lived with Gene's family after Gene had gone into the service. Bill recognized Gene from pictures and his birth mark on his face. Gene didn't remember Bill.

The birth mark was a mole on his right temple. His mom always believed that you could mark a baby. She said she saw a rat just before he was born and put her hands up to the side of her head.

Bill brought Gene home and we started going out. We all hung out at Joyce and Ricky's most of the time. We also spent lots of time with Gene's buddy John and his family. Gene got a good job at GM as a night supervisor. We were only dating but not serious at this time so I was still going to the dances with my friends.

Mom, Bill & Grandma Johnson

John's family were moving to Corona, California which was farther away for Gene to drive to work. He asked my mom if he could move in with us. I liked the idea of having someone else help with the rent. I remember my mom telling me that Gene was in love with me and didn't like my going out without him.

One weekend a Sailor I had danced with and I had given my address to showed up on a Saturday morning and Gene was home. Gene got upset and I asked the Sailor to leave. He said he would after he smoked his cigarette.

Meantime, Gene got up and dressed and started washing his car. The sailor helped him wash the car. It was a '52 Chevy, blue and white, nice car. After they finished, Gene told the sailor he would give him a ride and buy him a beer for helping him. They left together and didn't ask me to go along. After several hours, they returned together. Gene had had too much to drink. The sailor held his drink a little better. I made them some coffee and after Gene sobered up some, he and I drove the sailor to where he could get a ride back to the base. We never saw him again.

Jo Ann arriving in Califonia, 1952

After that incident, Gene asked me to marry him or else he was leaving and going back to Missouri. I accepted. We picked out a ring and drove to the beach. While we were sitting there, a cop approached the car. He asked if I was ok. I said, "Yes!" We had just gotten engaged. The cop told us to stay parked in that spot and he wouldn't bother us again.

After we got engaged, Gene wanted to go home to Missouri. He hadn't seen his family since he had gotten out of the Navy. Mom wanted to go back to Missouri too. David was starting to get into trouble. We had put him in a home run by the Optimist Clubs in California. They helped boys who were getting into trouble but not going to a reform school yet.

Sally was becoming a teenager too and looking at boys which also worried mom.

Robert had gotten discharged and he and Beva had moved back to Missouri. Mom wanted to be near them and see the baby grow up. Gene and I decided we would go back to Missouri to be married so our family and friends could come to the wedding. We both quit good jobs and took our last pay checks to make the trip home, with no jobs waiting for us there.

It never crossed our minds that we might not get another job.

Mom & Beva at Grandma's House 1954

Gene rented a small trailer and we took as much of our stuff as we could. We took David out of the home. We later would regret this. He was doing pretty good there and going to school.

Gene had to drive all the way, as, I didn't have a driver's license. We didn't want to spend our limited money on a motel. We would just stop on the side of the road and he would rest for a while, then go on.

When we got to New Mexico, we all got food poisoning from some bologna sandwiches. The weather was very hot. Gene was really sick and this scared all of us since none of us could drive. After throwing up and sleeping, he felt better so we continued on. That was the worst experience we had on that trip.

Trip Back to Missouri 1954

I have a hard time remembering the arrival in Missouri. I know Gene went to stay with his sister and her family until we were married. We must have stayed with Beva and Robert at Mrs. Edney's until we found a place of our own.

A place of our own was an old house made from a boat on the outskirts of Kimmswick by the Mississippi River. I am not sure if it had indoor plumbing or not. It was a roof over our heads. Not even sure if we paid rent or not. We had come full circle, back to living in abandon houses.

I went to United Van Lines and begged for my old job back and they were happy to have me back. Gene got a good job right away at an electric company but he had to join the union and pay union dues.

We found a better house to rent from an old friend of Gene's mom, in Kimmswick. It was another old place that needed painting and cleaning. So, on weekends we started to work on it with the help of our family.

BACK IN KIMMSWICK-PLANNING OUR WEDDING in 1954

We began to save and plan for our wedding.

Living in the boathouse was cramped and hot that summer. No air conditioning, only fans. We had forgotten how the humidity of the Midwest made the temperature feel twenty degrees hotter than it actually was. We really missed the weather of southern California. We also missed being able to go to the ocean to swim, being able to get to stores, and the public transportation we had in California.

The only way to the city of St. Louis was to walk a mile to the highway and wait on a Greyhound bus or hope someone from Kimmswick would stop and give a ride, if they were going into town. I still didn't drive or have a car. Gene had tried to teach me to drive before we left California. When he decided I was ready to drive in traffic and I had to make a right turn, I asked him if I could go right on a red light. He said yes, so I did. He didn't say I had to stop and make sure it was clear first. Fortunately, no accident or ticket resulted, but that ended in an argument and ended my driving lessons.

I had managed to get a ride into town with the Grimshaws again to get to work. Not having transportation was especially hard on Mom. Gene was living about ten miles away at his sister's. He had his car so he didn't have to deal with these problems.

Sally and David were ok and had some of their old friends back, although they, being from California, were not treated the same by some. Some people in Missouri did not like people from California or other places. For whatever reasons, people don't like outsiders. I have never understood this behavior. It is the same as being racist. If Sally and David talked about having more fun in California, the other kids would act like they thought we thought we were better or bragging. If they did the latest dances like the Bop that no one was doing in the Midwest at that time, some of the kids would call them queers.

California was known to accept the abnormal behavior of "queers", as they were called then, before any of the other U.S. states did. The film industry had a lot to do with the acceptance of immoral behavior. Things as we had known them were changing rapidly. Not just in California but everywhere.

By late September, 1955, Gene and I had set the date for our wedding as October 1st. We had rented one side of a house in Kimmswick by the river. It had been vacant for a long time and needed lots of repairs and painting. We worked on it after work and weekends with the help of David, and Sally and Gene's brother, Jerry. We had it almost ready to move into by the wedding date.

Phyllis JoAnn Bainter

Eugene J. Antoine

Mrs. Elizabeth Bailey
requests the honour of your presence at the
marriage ceremony of her daughter
Phyllis
to
Mr. Eugene J. Antoine
on Saturday, the first of October
nineteen hundred and fifty-five
at eleven o'clock in the morning
St. Joseph's Catholic Church
Kimmswick, Mo.

There were the usual bridal showers with friends and family. The best one was the one Gene's mom had for me. It was with all her friends, older women. They hand made so many nice things, crocheted doilies, dresser scarves, embroidered pillow cases and sheets, dish towels, and table cloths, all beautiful hand work. They all gave me great advice too like never let the sun set on an argument. This has always been one of my favorite memories.

Planning a wedding with divorces on both sides of the family is not easy.

I cannot explain why kids seem to think the divorce has nothing to do with them. Or why they want a relationship with the absent parent, especially when the absent parent pays little or no attention to them otherwise.

The kids feel their parents, after a while, should be able to leave their past behind for these special occasions, but that rarely happens.

I have come to realize how unfair it is to put anyone's feeling before the feelings of the parent who stayed and raised the children. Especially when the absent parent, in most cases, didn't even send support money.

Gene's sister wanted to have a wedding breakfast at her house and a reception afterwards. I was not wanting any reception because I didn't want everyone using our wedding as an excuse to get drunk. We agreed to buy one keg of beer and let them party.

The wedding breakfast went well. Gene's dad had agreed not to bring his wife so Gene's mom could be there. His wife Marie had been Gene's mom's best friend. Gene's mom had caught the two of them in bed in her own house. Which was the reason they had divorced. So, there was not ever going to be a time they could all celebrate any family functions together.

I was on pins and needles just having his dad and mom in the same room for this breakfast. However they both behaved and it went well. His dad even came to the wedding alone, thank God.

My father was living in Indiana and I hadn't seen him for a long time. He came to Kimmswick before the wedding. He was such a jerk that I didn't ask him to give me away. After all, he had given me away a long time before this.

I asked my sister's husband Robert to do that for me and he was thrilled to do it. We asked Sally to be my maid of honor and Gene's brother Jerry to be best man. We asked our friends Alvin, Paul, Eileen, Paul's sister and Phyllis Vitito to be the bridal party.

No wedding ever goes as planned. The day of the wedding, Eileen broke out in hives so bad she had to go to the emergency room. Paul wasn't in the wedding either. He and his wife Jackie did come to the wedding though.

St. Joseph's Catholic Church

I had gotten a really bad cold and had laryngitis so I could barely speak above a whisper, but did manage the "I Do".

Eugene and Joann Antoine Wedding, October 1, 1955

Our friend Vernon Kraemer, Ma Green's grandson was an usher. He also was the driver and owner of the 1954 red Mercury convertible we drove around in. It was a beautiful car. Vernon was always clowning. He had gotten a big box of suckers so when anyone yelled "sucker" to us, we threw a handful of suckers to them. After driving all over town with all our friends following us blowing their horn. We finally went back to Sis's for the reception.

It went nicely, lots of good food. We didn't stay very long because we still had no idea of where we were going to spend that night. It would be at some motel so we at least would be alone. Certainly, there was no honeymoon planned as we barely had the money for the wedding.

We drove west out of St. Louis and finally around dark we started looking for a motel. They were few and far between at this point. Finally, Gene said no matter what the next one looked like, it was where we were stopping. I would have just kept driving.

We did find a small privately owned motel and it was getting very cold. The owner came into the room with us and lit the floor furnace. This was under a grate in the floor. I had never seen one like it. He never mentioned that it got hot to the touch. I suppose he gave us credit for having that much sense. Wrong! The bathroom had no door to separate it from the bedroom. Gene had to help get the buttons undone on my dress which I would have never been able to do without his help. There must have been fifty of those little covered buttons down the back of the dress. I remember trying to finish undressing and getting into my negligee in the far corner of the bathroom so he wouldn't see me undress. As I hurried to the bed to get under the covers, I forgot about the furnace and by now it was HOT. I burnt the bottom of my foot. I won't bore you with the rest of the wedding night details except to say it was not a pleasant experience for either of us. But love conquers all and makes life bearable. Thank God.

The next morning, we drove back to Sis's to pick up our gifts and help her clean up. Beva was there helping and, of course, tried her best to embarrass me. She succeeded.

We stayed in the boathouse from October until just before Christmas. It was miserable cold. We only had a wood stove for heat. Every morning Gene would get up first and build the fire, which went out almost every night. It got cold really quick. We had been spoiled in California with gas furnaces which rarely had to be lit.

Before we could get the house finished in Kimmswick, Gene's mom told us we could move upstairs in her flat in the city. This made more sense to us. Mom wanted to find a job and it would be closer for Gene and me to get to work. So that is what we did just after we were married.

We moved to St Louis and we once again had a gas furnace and inside plumbing. It was cramped and lacked privacy. Gene and I had never had much privacy. You don't miss what you never had. Having an inside bathroom was the ultimate luxury. With a real bathtub, we were in heaven. There was only one bedroom, which Gene and I had because we were married.   Mom, Sally and David slept in the living room on couches or daybeds. The daybeds or roll-a-way beds, as they were called, folded up in the middle and could just be stored away in a corner. Fortunately, the rooms in these old houses were very big.

We had just moved in and had our first Christmas there, when Gene got laid off from his job and I found out I was pregnant. Things were not looking good.

Gene and Paul Weber both were laid off and the only job they could find was making children's swing sets for $1.37 an hour. Both had been making about $4.00 an hour so this was almost humiliating. Paul's wife Jackie was pregnant also.

We spent most of our time with Paul and Jackie since he and Gene had both gotten out of the Navy. One evening while we were playing cards, Gene and Paul told us they were going to re-enlist in the service. Jackie and I had no objections. It was better than always being laid off. Most people we knew lived from lay off to lay off.

People who worked as laborers had to always be prepared as a laborer that this was coming. No one we knew ever seemed to get ahead. They would make good money and live ok for a while, but then have to spend what they saved when they were laid off.

Gene's two older brothers had already decided to make careers out of the military. Both were doing ok and liked that lifestyle. After talking to his brothers, Gene and Paul decided to go Air Force because men had to be gone from home more in the Navy.

ON THE ROAD AGAIN: JOINING THE U.S. AIR FORCE-1956

With Christmas over, no decent job offers coming and expecting our first baby, our decision was made. Gene would go into the U.S.A.F. His brother was stationed in Manchester, New Hampshire. He told Gene if he came to New Hampshire to enlist he could be stationed with him at Pease Air Force Base.

After spending many years in the military, why his brother ever thought this would happen, I have never figured out. At any rate, he must have thought it to be true. As he had been in the service over ten years and was older than Gene, we believed he knew this to be a fact.

Since Gene and Paul would most likely get stationed in New Hampshire together, we decided the four of us would take what we could and make the trip together. That way, Jackie and I could look for a place for us to live while the guys took their training. I am not sure the guys even knew they would have to go to boot camp again and I think they thought if they did it would be in New Hampshire.

On about the twenty-fifth of February in the middle of winter, we started driving East. Not smart. Don't think either of us even had chains for our tires. We certainly did not have money for a motel. It was another of those trips driving straight through and praying we didn't have car troubles.

Our cars were fully loaded with the household goods we thought we would need. Paul was even pulling a small trailer. The weather was not too bad until we got into the Poconos mountains of Pennsylvania. There, we hit snow and fog.

We got there at night, of course. The guys were tired and neither of us girls had driver's licenses. Driving was so scary. We couldn't stop or pull off the road for fear we could not get started again.

By morning, things looked a little better. We could now see what we thought were mountains but were just long grades up and down without drop-offs on the sides. We got to Manchester, New Hampshire on the twenty-sixth of February. On the next day, the guys went to the recruiters and re-enlisted. When they came back to the house, we were told they had to leave the next morning to go to San Antonio, Texas. They would be taking their training there for the next six weeks. The next morning, we said our goodbyes and they were gone.

We were devastated. Neither Jackie nor I could call home for money to live on or go home on. We were stuck in New Hampshire, like it or not. Both of us being pregnant and unable to drive further worsened our situations.

Jackie and I would have to stay with Gene's brother and his family at least until the guys got paid. The Air Force paid once a month at this time.

Fran, Gene's brother and wife Jean had a little girl about four and a new baby boy. Thank God, they made room for us in their living room. All our things had to stay in the cars because they had no extra room and we couldn't afford a storage shed. I had only met Fran and Jean one time for a short visit when they came to Missouri before we were married. Jackie had never met them and we were both very uncomfortable intruding on their lives. I am sure this was not what they had in mind either, but we all made the best of a bad situation.

Gene wrote to me and I wrote to him every day. He sent me all the money he got except for the necessities he needed. Jackie wrote to Paul but Paul seldom wrote to her and didn't send her all the money he could have. Later, Gene told me Paul was going to the club on base and drinking some. He also had been hanging out with some of the girls on the base too. I sometimes heard Jackie crying in the night but she never talked to me about her worries. This short time together made us friends for the rest of our lives.

After the first month there, we talked to the landlady who lived downstairs. She rented us a bedroom in her apartment. That worked for about a month, but then her daughter didn't like us being there. We found another room in an old rooming house. With what money, we had between us, we usually could afford to go to the movies once a month on payday or stay home playing rummy. No tv, but we had a small radio and listened to all the soaps. As the weather got nicer, we were able to go for walks and look around the stores.

Gene had started teaching me to drive in California and he made sure I knew how to start the cars to keep the batteries charged. We did this about once a week and then one day I decided we could drive around town a little to practice so I could get my license when he got back. I never wanted to be so dependent on anyone again. We didn't see Fran and Jean much after we moved to the rooming house.

Jackie finally decided to go to the Red Cross and see if they could find out why Paul wasn't sending her more money. This really made Paul mad. His Commander had him explain it to him also. From then on, she got more money from him. The Air Force treated dependents better than the Navy. The Navy's policy concerning wives was, "You were not issued a wife in your Sea bag. Therefore she's your problem, not the Navy's."

After we talked to the Red Cross, they set up doctors' appointments for us. I had not yet gone to the doctor to find out when to expect this baby. Jackie was already about six months along. The hospital we had to go to was in Portsmouth, Maine and we had no way to get there. It was only about an hour drive, so the Red Cross sent an older man to take us for our appointments. It was a very nice day out. He loved driving us and even took us to lunch. It was one of the best times we had living in New Hampshire.

Finally, the six weeks were up and Gene was on his way back to New Hampshire to take us back home to Missouri. Gene had gotten his orders. He was not going to be stationed in New Hampshire or even close. He was going to Fairbanks, Alaska, to the very ends of the earth, we thought. He had a month to get us home and get to Alaska.

Gene took a bus from Texas, which took him about three days. He was so tired when he finally got to Manchester, New Hampshire. At least the Air Force gave him enough travel pay and time to get to Alaska. I think it was about three cents a mile. That really helped us out because, as luck would have it, Paul got no extra money for travel. He was being stationed right there in San Antonio, Texas.

Fran and Jean decided to take leave and help us get to Missouri. The only problem was that Jean did not drive either and we had Paul and Jackie's car there. Gene was just going to leave it there until Paul could come get it. I told him I had been driving the cars while he was gone and wanted to get my license now. If I passed I could drive their car home. He did not like this idea but took me to the DMV anyway. I am sure he thought I would fail. The man at the DMV was not going to pass me because I couldn't parallel park backing into a parking space. I cried and told him Gene was going to Alaska and I needed to be able to get myself to the doctors. He felt sorry for me and gave in. Of course, I never told him that I was driving all the way to Missouri the next day.

Our first day driving, I was a little scared and Gene was worrying a lot. The second day he was yelling at me for driving too fast. We made it to Missouri without an incident. Mom had stayed in the flat above Gene's mom so we were home again.

Jackie stayed with us until Paul got leave to come and get her after her baby was born.

Gene had a few days home and then packed and left for Alaska.

We weren't sure if I would be able to go there at that time. It would all depend on the Commander and money. The military would not let dependents go overseas unless they could show the Commander they would be able to live on the money they were paid. Alaska was considered an overseas assignment because it was still a territory, not a State.

I went to work for Kelly Girls, a temp agency, to make the money I needed to go to Alaska. No one would hire me for a permanent position because I was pregnant and they knew I would have to quit.

Gene got a job after work on the base. He set up trailers for those who moved in and out of the base trailer park. It was a good job through the summer but not in the Alaskan winters.

Jackie's time passed. We had a friends who lived on Scott Air Force Base at Bellville, Illinois. That was where we had to go to the doctors. It was about an hour by car so, as her time got close, she moved in with them.

While she was there she got a notice that Paul wasn't making the car payments and their car was going to be repossessed. I didn't want them to lose that car after I had gone through all the trouble of getting it back home for them. So, every day I moved the car to different spots in the neighborhood. Then Beva and I decided to take it to Jackie on the base. We didn't think the repo people could get on the base to get it. We got about half way to the base and blew a water hose. Thank God, Beva had been around Robert and old cars enough to know what it was and how to fix it. She repaired the hose and took out the spark plugs and dried them off, we got the hose back on. We made it to the base and got it to Jackie. We visited with Jackie, then headed for home. About a week later, Jackie told us our effort didn't help. The repo company was allowed on the base to claim the car. Lesson learned.

Paul got home after the baby was born and Jackie went back to

Texas with him.

After Gene left for Alaska, I stayed at home with Mom and the kids. During this time, Sally was getting more independent. She had been babysitting earning her own money. She wasn't happy in school and just wanted to go to work and spend what time she could in Kimmswick. She became more rebellious as a teenager does and had many arguments with Mom.

David was not doing well either and getting into trouble. He was washing a car for a neighbor when he decided to take it for a ride with no license. The guy reported it stolen and David was sent to a reform school for a year. Mom's health was not good. She had to be hospitalized for a hysterectomy. When she left the hospital, she didn't have a ride home or money for a bus so she walked. She was readmitted to the hospital for a blocked intestine and almost died. I was worried to leave her but she insisted I go to be with Gene. Beva and Sally were close by so I did leave.

The thought just came to me that all I have written about to this point happened before I was twenty-one years old.

Paul stayed in the service until he retired from the Air Force in Austin, Texas. He and Jackie stayed married for over fifty years. Though Paul was never the husband she deserved, Jackie never gave up on him. They had three boys. Paul had a dump truck business and did very well financially.

Paul's health failed a couple of years ago; he had to go on oxygen. Jackie had died a few years previously. Paul called me shortly before Gene died. He was very unhappy but I could never have guessed what he had planned to do. He drove his truck out into the country and shot himself in the head. It was very sad for his boys. I guess he didn't want to be alone.

* * *

CHAPTER SIX- ALASKA 1956-59

Finally, about June, 1956, Gene had found an apartment we could afford and the Commander gave us the ok for me to come to Alaska. On the twelfth of June, 1956, I borrowed fifty dollars from my father-in-law so I could afford to fly to Fairbanks, Alaska, to be with Gene. Gene's dad was the only person we knew that we could borrow from, and who even had fifty dollars. Which, by the way, we paid back two and a half years later when we returned from Alaska.

Gene had just earned his first stripe, A/3 Class. This was one step up the pay ladder and gave us fifty dollars more a month to live on. Our total pay was a little over three hundred dollars a month. The Air Force did not increase your pay for a wife but did give you a little more for the first child only. Gene had a break in service of over one year and he lost all his rank from the Navy. They did count his time towards retirement.

This was my first time to fly. I left St. Louis going to Seattle on a small prop plane on a small airline called Braniff Airlines. They served us a meal which I remember vividly. It was Filet Mignon, another first. I have had many Filet Mignons since then but never as good. I transferred planes in Seattle for Fairbanks. I don't remember much about that flight. I probably slept.

Gene had borrowed a car and met me. The land was barren, no sign of life until we arrived in Fairbanks. Fairbanks was not a thriving metropolis in 1956. Alaska was still a Territory and had not yet become a State. The only thing I remember about that drive was a dead moose on the side of the road.

Home was not a modern duplex but just an old house or cabin divided into two-room apartments. However, we did have a bathroom inside. There were other GI's living there also, in small camp trailers. They had to go to a community shower and bathroom so, we were still on middle income living scale.

Fairbanks was twenty-six miles from the base where Gene was stationed at Eielson AFB and we had no car. Other guys living in Fairbanks were stationed at Eielson so Gene figured he could get a ride to the base. He hadn't considered the winter coming and how very cold Alaska was in the winter to hitchhike.

As part of our rent, we had to keep the fire in the furnace going for the two apartments, plus shovel the snow off the roof. If it got too heavy, it might collapse the roof. I let the fire go out one time and I never did that again. I could not shovel the roof because I was pregnant so Gene had to do that also.

Gene wasn't always able to find a ride to the base and had to hitchhike that twenty-six miles several times, in the first winter. He would leave the house at 3:00 a.m. because he could not be late and sometimes he would not get home until 6:00 p.m. or later.

Those were long, cold, lonely days. I missed home a lot. We had no radio, tv or money for entertainment. We had a deck of cards. We played cribbage, solitaire, and rummy. If we could find another couple, we played pinochle until the baby came that October.

After the baby came, the days seemed a lot shorter and fuller. I had to keep the fire going, both in summer and winter if we were to have hot water. I had a full day and many new experiences for both baby and me to deal with just learning how to take care of a baby by myself.

Neither Gene nor I, as teenagers, had been around babies and there were no phone calls home to ask Mom. No phone either. By the time the letters with advice got to us we had already had to figure out what we had to do. I prayed a lot and cried a little. I didn't have time to get "cabin fever" as they called depression those days.

In the other apartment attached to ours was another young Air Force couple from North Carolina. They had a new baby, their first too. We didn't visit but talked when we saw each other coming or going. I guess, being new parents and away from home, they were having a lot of new learning experiences too. They did have a car but I never saw her drive it.

One day in late September, I had a doctor's appointment and had to leave early because I had to walk to the base in Fairbanks, about two and a half miles. The base was Ladd AFB. It later would become an Army base called Fort Wainwright. There were Army guys stationed there at this time. It was not a bad walk if you were not eight months pregnant.

The weather was not too bad yet, but I had to make sure the fire would stay lit while I was gone. That day I checked the fire. It was fine and I put extra wood on it and left. I got to my appointment ok and was so happy I had not gained any weight. The Air force nurse that checked us in and took our weight was like a Drill Sergeant and yelled at those who did gain too much weight. We were only allowed to gain twenty pounds those days. I was very intimidated, as were most of the young wives new to the military life. Our husbands had to obey orders and we felt we did too, even though the military person was the only one that would be disciplined. We didn't want to make trouble for our husbands. Some girls would leave these appointments in tears.

I arrived back to the apartment only to find the fire had gone out. It was getting colder. I had to rebuild the fire for the first time. I found some paper and put the wood on it and lit the paper which burnt really well, but the wood did not. This must have taken me an hour or more before I could even get one piece of wood to burn. Finally, it started when I was frustrated to the point of crying. I was really perturbed at the girl next door, because she had just crawled into bed with her baby to stay warm and didn't even try to restart the fire before I got back. It wasn't her job.

I went into my apartment and started cleaning house. Remember, I am now eight months pregnant.

The bathroom was an afterthought in this apartment. It was the size of a closet. The door opened in with the shower behind the door. The sink was on the other wall sticking out so I almost had to suck in my stomach to get by it to get to the toilet, which was next to the shower in the corner.

I got down on my hands and knees to scrub the toilet and mop the floor around it. When I reached up and flushed the toilet, steam came up out of the toilet. The hot water heater next to the sink began to make a loud noise as if like it might explode. I got up as fast as a pregnant woman could and turned on the faucets, but all that came out was steam. I ran to the kitchen and turned on the faucets there, again only steam. The house was like a sauna but I didn't know what the word sauna meant in those days. Finally, water started to trickle out and the pipes cooled down.

I was unaware that the cold-water pipes were placed close to the hot water lines to keep them from freezing. I guess there was no thermostat on the water heater and I had gotten the fire so hot it caused all this to happen. I do not have to tell you that by the time Gene got home from work that day, I was in tears and ready to pack and go home to Mama. Gene calmed me down and I learned it was better to let the fire die than to pile too much wood on it.

On October 1st, 1956, we celebrated our first anniversary. We had no money for gifts so we made each other a card. I bought Gene a toy car. I wrote this poem to Gene.

"If I had lots of money, Honey,
A brand-new car I'd buy for you.
But since we have no money, Honey,
This little car will have to do"

I signed it, "Love you real whole lots". This is the way we signed all our cards to each other from the time we started to date and throughout for the fifty-five years we were married. Bad grammar, not very elegant, but it said it all.

On October 23rd, 1956, I awoke and realized things had changed and I needed to go to the hospital. Not sure why Gene was home, but like all first parents, we were in a panic. First of all, we had no car or phone.

Gene went next door and asked to borrow their car. They said yes. We got to the hospital and I felt fine, no pains. The doctor examined me. He would have sent us home but, since we had no car, he decided to admit me. He told Gene he might as well go back home as this baby would probably not come today. Gene had to take the car back so he left and I stayed.

The doctor was right. It was 5:00 p.m. before I ever had a pain. I had laid there all day as many other women came and went. I remember, one girl prayed the Our Father and Hail Mary over and over. I didn't know what to expect. The pain finally got more intense. Gene had not returned. I didn't know if he had found a phone and called the hospital. At around 6:00 p.m., I finally was in the delivery room and had my first baby, a girl. Gene finally came in around 7:00 p.m., apologizing for not being there. It didn't matter now. I was fine and so was the baby.

I had not had a bad time except for the pains and felt fine now with the pain killer called a spinal or saddle block they had given me for delivery. I got up and walked with him to the nursery, about three rooms down the hall to see Victoria Lynn, as we had decided to name her. Gene left and I went to sleep.

Vicky in Alaska - 1957

When they brought the baby to me for the first time to feed her and I sat up, I felt as though the top of my head became un-attached. It was the worst pain I had ever remembered. I called the nurse and asked her to feed the baby a bottle. The nurse got upset with me because I had said I was going to breast feed her. I said that plan was made before I knew what to expect. Finally, she agreed to feed the baby and I tried to sleep. Something else happened that I hadn't expected. When the milk comes in, it hurts. Now I have the severe headache and this new pain. Trying to hold this baby was impossible.

I wanted my Mom.

The doctor finally came in and prescribed codeine for the pain. I could have kissed the nurse after I got that first little pill. The headache came because I had gotten up too soon after the saddle block, a new type of shot for delivery. Women were not even to use a pillow or move for the first 24 hours after taking this shot. Why did no one tell me this?

By the time the pain quit, I had decided not to bother with breast feeding. It was enough to just get up so many times with this baby who seemed to only sleep an hour at a time. Gene was willing to get up and help, but he was still having to hitchhike to the base in the cold and not getting home till after dinner time. By the time I got him awake, it was easier just to get up myself. I guess, because I was not comfortable being a mom, the baby cried all the time she was awake. We were stuck in these two rooms alone because it was winter in Alaska.

You don't go for a walk when it is twenty below zero outside. I didn't have time for postpartum blues or after-birth blues, as it was known then but I know it does exist.

It was Christmas time. One evening Gene decided he would try to chop down a small tree for us. He put on his parka and took the small hatchet he had brought home from his tool box at work and went to look for a tree. He was gone maybe a half hour. He came in almost frozen with no tree. We resigned ourselves to not having even a tree that year.

We felt alone and missed family even more.

The couple next door was moving. They had gotten a more modern apartment. They wanted to sell their small tv. We had gotten a small raise when the baby came so we decided to buy their tv instead of going to the movies. With the baby, the movies were not something we could sit through any way. When they brought the tv over. They also had a tree about one foot tall with a string of lights and some homemade decorations on it. They gave it to us. Things were looking up.

Gene bought me a necklace with a Catholic miraculous medal and Vicky a little stuffed dog. It played a lullaby as the tail went around to make the dog roll over. I couldn't get to a store to get him anything. I felt bad but he said he had all he wanted. He was always so easy to please.

When spring came, we had finally moved up on the list to get a decent apartment in off-base housing. This was a step up in our world. We finally had other friends in the complex and Gene had found a regular ride to work. No more fire to take care of.

Life was so much better for both of us. Now I had friends with children that I could enjoy and share experiences with. I became a much calmer mom. The baby also changed and seemed to be happier. She was learning to walk and had other little ones to play with and learn from.

Jo Ann and Vicky, Alaska

Life was good. We were happy. We started back to church together. I wanted Vicky to be baptized. I went to talk to the priest, Father Babb. After Mass, I asked Father Babb if he would bless my baby until I could have her baptized. Father Babb told me blessings do not take the place of baptism. He asked why I felt we had to wait. I said I had no money for the dress or the priest.

Father Babb took Vicky from my arms and said, "We will baptize her right now." This was not as I had thought it should be. Not pretty, as she had already spit up on her dress and we both smelled like puke, but she was baptized. Father Babb would come to our apartment when he could and give us instructions in our faith. He realized that Gene and I had no idea what the Catholic faith was about. We claimed to be Catholic simply because our parents had us baptized, even though they didn't go to the church either. That is why the church has gotten so careful about baptisms and wants the parents to be active and know the religion they want to pass on to their children. I think it is wrong to withhold baptism for that reason because Gene and I would probably have had no faith at all if not baptized as infants.

Father Babb became our friend and mentor for the rest of his life. We only visited with him one time after our years in Alaska, on a trip we made in 1979. He was in a home for old priests in Biloxi, Mississippi. He died there. We wrote to him only at Christmas time but he was very important to my life as a Catholic.

When I finally made the move to accept Christ and a religion. I never felt I could be anything but a Catholic. I went to lots of different churches with my friends over the years but always knew I would stay a Catholic.

When Vicky was seven months old, I found out I was pregnant again. Our son, Jim was born in January, 1958. Just a year before, Alaska became a state on January 3, 1959.

This pregnancy was different from the first. We had moved into a two-bedroom apartment and we were doing quite well. We were able to buy a car. It was an old Studebaker from some Airman leaving Alaska. He knew it could not make it down the

Alcan Highway. The highway to Alaska via Canada at that time was not a paved road, gravel all the way. We didn't worry about driving this old car back to the states.

We were afraid to even drive it out of Fairbanks. At least we could now go to the commissary for groceries without depending on our more affluent neighbors. Also, Gene had been promoted to A/1C, which was more money. We were even able to buy a washing machine. In our first apartment, we had only a wash tub in the furnace room and a broom stick for an agitator which Gene used to wash his heavy uniforms and work clothes. We now set our goal to save for a new car when we got home again.

The months passed and Jim was born, January 31st, 1958. Not at all like our first baby, he had problems. He was severely club-footed, both feet. I remember telling the doctor in delivery how Gene's mom believed a mother could mark a baby. She said Gene's birthmark happened because she saw a rat just before he was born. I found it so ironic that Gene's first boy would be club-footed because all the boys in Kimmswick had nicknamed Gene "Clubby" when he kicked a football through the church window at St Joseph's church. That was the church we were married in.

The doctor, of course, laughed at me. He didn't have a better answer for the club-footedness but assured me Jim would be ok. The medical profession had come a long way in the research and correction of this disability. We were lucky, too, because we had an orthopedic doctor on staff.

I had lost a lot of blood so I had to have a blood transfusion. Jim had a heart murmur too. The doctor didn't seem to be worried so I relaxed, thinking all would be ok. The nurse came in after I was back in my room with the baby so we could see him. She said, "They do such great things with this now. Why, in five years you won't even know there is anything wrong." Five years?

That really upset me to think about the next five years and what this baby would have to endure. One of the corpsman, Seibert, a young man about nineteen or twenty who helped in the delivery room, came every day to hold Jim and help me feed him.

The doctor had put casts on both of Jim's feet by the time he was fourteen hours old. The casts made him heavy so the nurses would pick him up and hand him to me. They had to change the casts weekly as he grew. I had to stay seven days in the hospital because I was so anemic.

Gene had to rely on neighbors to watch Vicky so he could come to the hospital and go to work. We had made great friends with Peggy and Jack Corbin. If we left the doors open between our apartments, it was like living together. So, Vicky was as much at home at Peg's as she was at our home. Peg and Jack had three 3 little girls and she was pregnant with her fourth child. They were from South Carolina. I loved Peg's southern accent. Peg was such a help to me because she was a little older and had more experience with kids.

One summer day we all went on a picnic. It actually was picnic weather in Alaska. Peg had purchased an old-fashioned ice cream freezer and we made homemade peach ice cream. Jack ask Peg how much the freezer had cost her. She said something like fifteen dollars and Jack got upset at the amount she spent on it.

Peg answered him back and said, "Well, hell, Jack. If I knew you were going to make such a fuss, I would have told you a ten dollar lie." We all laughed at that. So did Jack. They, too, became lifelong friends of ours until Peggy died in the 1980's. They returned to Ninety-Six, South Carolina after they retired from the army.

The first day home with Jim, I expected Vicky to run to me and be happy to see me and the new baby. She didn't. She wouldn't even let me hold her. She was a very independent child and happy to go play with the girls next door. It hurt my feelings thinking she had gotten along so well without me. She was more loving the next day. I think she was upset that I had gone away and feared I might go away again.

Jim grew and was healthy and normal other than his feet. The heart murmur went away by his six-week checkup just as the doctor had said it would. We took him weekly for his cast changes. This became a problem as he was terrified of the sound the saw made when they cut the old cast off. At first this scared me too until the doctor told us it wouldn't cut the skin. It just vibrated the cast apart.

We had a hard time holding Jim still so the new cast could be put on. The doctor tried holding Jim's feet still to wrap the cast and keep the feet in the right position until they dried. It was almost impossible. We learned with a second doctor how this procedure could have been made so simple.

Dr. Tom Powers was our second doctor, in Montana. He was not a military doctor. He wrapped the casting cloth around the feet and sent us home. He told us to come back the next day after the cast set up. He then cut around the ankle and was able to put the foot right where he wanted it because it was solid. Then he simply wrapped more casting tape around it, let it dry, and it was done until the next change. As Jim got olde,r he sometimes would kick his heels against the floor, breaking the cast and we would have to go back and do it all over again.

They didn't want to make the cast to heavy because it would be harder on his muscles to move his legs and also made it harder for us to carry him around.

Many of our friends were now getting ready to rotate or leave Alaska. The base radio station would announce who had orders and where they were going. Our friends, the Hoppers, found out they were going to Great Falls, Montana. Montana and North Dakota were the two bases no one wanted to go to after serving in Alaska. Sometimes the winters there were colder than Alaska.

We found out about a week later that we, too, were being sent to Montana. We tried to get our orders changed to somewhere closer to Missouri, but that didn't happen.

We left Alaska in late November, 1958. We flew to Washington State on an Air Force plane, then took a commercial flight to St. Louis. It was an unusually warm winter. There were still house-flies in the airport which fascinated Vicky and Jim. They chased them, trying to catch them.

I don't think they had seen houseflies in Alaska. No houseflies but there were mosquitos big enough to carry off a small child! That's an exaggeration. Sounds like a Texas Big-story tale but they were the biggest mosquitos we had ever seen.

When we got home to Missouri, my mom was still living in the apartment above Gene's mom.

David was back home and doing ok. When he and Mom were not getting along, he would stay downstairs with Lou and Art. They didn't mind his being there. Lou could get David to do things Mom couldn't. They had a special relationship. Lou tolerated David doing things that she would have killed her boys for doing. They made each other laugh and she liked having him around.

Sally had run off twice to get married to Don Howard, but both times she backed out and came home.

Finally, they did go to the court house and got married. She had a little boy, Donnie, by the time we came home. Don was very controlling, but they had their own apartment and Mom was alone most of the time.

While we were in Alaska, Lou wrote to Gene to tell him a tree limb had fallen on the '52 Chevy. We had to leave the car with them while we were gone. Gene was upset when he saw the car even though, being an auto-body repairman now, he could have easily fixed it. He decided to trade it in instead. He always regretted this decision since old cars got to be collector items later. He had already decided to buy a new car and the Chevy would not have been a good family car. It had only two doors, making it hard to load and unload babies. We knew we were expecting our third baby by this time. I didn't go with him to buy the new car because I didn't want to have Mom or Lou take care of the babies. Jim was still in casts and heavy even for me to lift and carry. He was crawling everywhere. The casts never slowed him down. He was pulling up and trying to stand up. Vicky was a little mother. She ran for everything he wanted.

Gene came home with a 1958 Ford Galaxy, grey and bright yellow, very flashy. I was concerned he would be an impulsive buyer like his mom.

Lula didn't go out shopping much but many salesmen came to the house. The coffee salesman from Jewel Tea Company, the Watkins man who sold everything from household goods to spices and medicines, the Fuller Brush Man who sold brooms, vacuum cleaners and cleaning supplies, and the insurance men. She had bought policies on everyone in the family, including my mom. This was all before Avon. She should have owned stock in that company.

Once, when we were first married, she went shopping with Gene and me to buy me a new coat. The Man-made furs were the newest thing in coats. I did not want a fur coat but she and Gene were set on my having one. I guess Gene wanted people to know we were able to afford this coat. Lula found some shiny sequined hats to go with the coat which I finally said no to. I remember Gene saying to her, "Mom, if shit shined, you would buy it." We all laughed at the thought. I did get the fur coat and wore it for many years.

Our new Ford had four doors. This made it easier to get the kids in and out but I worried they would play with the door handles and maybe open the doors while we were driving. There were no child locks or car seats back then. Gene was happy with his choice and proud that he finally had credit good enough to buy a new car.

This was the first big debt we had, $1500.00. It worried me some to be that far in debt, but Gene had worked so hard and he deserved to have the car of his choice. He hardly ever bought anything for himself.

When our leave was over and it was time for us to go to Montana, we convinced Mom to come with us.

We would now have three babies and Mom would be a great help. Her health had worsened too. It would help us both.

* * *

CHAPTER SEVEN-MONTANA AND GROWING FAMILY 1959-62

We left St. Louis for Montana. We had room for some of Mom's things that we might need to set up house-keeping. We had left Alaska with nothing but our clothes and what belongings we could bring on the airplane plus the two new additions to our family. After loading the car and saying our goodbyes. Leaving David who was now eighteen with Lou and Art, Gene's parents, we started on our new adventure to the Wild West, Montana.

The weather was good for this trip, an unusually warm winter being January, 1959. We didn't even have to wear coats in Missouri. The trip was uneventful and full of great scenery. Mom and Vicky in the back seat were getting to know each other. These were the days before car seats so I had Jim in the front seat most of the time. He was still in casts on both legs but he had learned to crawl and pull up.

We checked in at Malmstrom AFB. The bases in the Air Force had household goods, like dishes sheets, etc. We could check them out to use until we were settled at our new place and our belongings arrived. This was a great help. The base also set up a sponsor to help you find housing and had lists of apartments for rent that the bases checked out. We were also lucky that our friend, Chuck Hopper and his family, who had been stationed with us in Alaska, were already living there. They were a great help. We found a very nice apartment right away. It was in a private home. It was in the basement that had been converted into an apartment. There were with only two bedrooms but the living room was large and L-shaped. One end was about 12x12 so we hung a sliding door divider and made a bedroom for Mom out of it. We had a nice fenced-in yard in the back for the kids to play in. We put our name on the list for base housing but housing was issued according to time in service and rank. It was not likely we would get it anytime soon.

We settled in and looked forward to the time we would spend in Great Falls. The Hoppers had two little girls and the kids all got along really well. We spent most weekends with them. Sometimes I would keep the Hopper girls overnight so the parents could go out. We didn't have money to go out with them. That winter got very cold in Montana, down to fifty-four below zero at one point, colder than Alaska. We were not going out with two babies in that.

Mom found a job in a restaurant because she didn't want to take anything from us. The restaurant was in a neighboring area of Great Falls called Black Eagle, near the Indian reservation. This was the true West with probably the first real Indians we had ever had contact with. They were not wild as we had always envisioned them from the movies. In fact, sometimes I had to be told they were Indian. Many did not live on the reservations. They lived, like us, in the community.

Gene was still working in the evenings for extra money. He could take the cars he worked on, doing body work, to the base auto-hobby shop. They had all the tools he needed and even a paint booth. He could make more money in one evening than we were making all month from the Air Force.

Life was good and I didn't have to go to work.

We didn't have an orthopedic doctor for Jim at this base. We were going to try to get a compassionate transfer to Scott AFB, Illinois. Scott AFB is still has a regional hospital and has more specialists. It was also close to the Shriners hospital in St. Louis and home.

Meantime, the base doctors helped us to find a local doctor and Crippled Children's helped with the cost. Fortunately, Dr. Thomas Powers was considered one of the top orthopedic doctors in the country. He agreed to treat Jim. I hope he did get paid. Every time I asked about the bill he said he would take care of the paperwork. He never sent us a bill.

The first time he changed Jim's cast, I thought he did not know what he was doing. He simply wrapped both legs and feet in the casting gauze, just as they were. Then told me to come back the next day. Which we did. The next day he took the cast saw, cut the cast at the ankle, put the foot in the position he wanted, and re-wrapped more of the casting gauze around the cut. So, simple and so easy because, no matter how the baby kicked and fought, you, you had the foot stayed contained. I realized the first doctor could have corrected Jim's feet so much faster, if he had only known this technique. We were so happy with this doctor we decided not to transfer.

After a couple of months, my sister Sally called. We had our first phone. Moving on up in the world. Sally wanted to leave her husband Don because he drank and would get physically abusive to her and the baby. I told her she could come and stay with us until she knew what she wanted to do. She took a Greyhound bus. It was a long hard trip from Missouri to Montana with a baby. Buses did not have bathrooms on them so you had to make do, changing babies. She was distraught by the time we picked her and the baby up at the bus station. The baby had gotten sick and spit up on them both. I felt so sorry for her.

A few weeks after arriving, she found out she was pregnant again. She found a job and started saving money to go back home. She was becoming more and more unhappy. Don called her all the time, wanting her to come home. He promised not to drink and make their life better. Finally, she agreed to go home. She could see life was not going to be easy with just one baby and having two, would be impossible. Don got his vacation and drove to Montana to get them and take them home.

Life got somewhat back to normal for us again. Spring came. Montana was a paradise for a fisherman and Gene loved to fish. We spent most of our free weekends going on fishing trips and picnics with the Hoppers. It was great fun for all of us.

One Sunday, we were going to meet the Hoppers and bring their girls to them, then go on a picnic. We had just pulled away from their house with them in front of us. As we were passing a church that had just ended its service, a little boy about six, suddenly ran in front of the Hoppers' car. He could not avoid hitting the boy. It was devastating. Of course, there was an investigation and the base had to investigate also. Hopper was cleared. It was not his fault but he still suffered from the accident. I was always so thankful that we were not in front of them and that we had all the kids in our car. I am not sure the kids ever knew what happened. Hopper asked for a transfer shortly after this and got it. We had no contact with them after they left Montana.

We had made friends with another couple, Floyd and Donna Marks. They had two kids, Craig and a cute little girl, Sandy. Floyd and Gene got along really well. They liked fishing and hunting together. Donna and I got along ok even though we were not at all alike. Like us, they didn't have money to go out much and we all liked playing cards. It was good entertainment and free. We could do this while the kids played together. We took turns going to each other's houses and making new desserts and exchanging babysitting. We spent almost every weekend together.

The time passed and I had our third child, Gina. The pregnancy and delivery were normal and she had nothing wrong with her feet. She was perfect. Of course, by this time I was a more relaxed mom so this baby was a joy. Mom was still with us and was such a big help. She would get up in the night and take care of Gina.

After Gina was born, I decided to find a job and have Mom baby-sit for me. We were doing good money-wise, but I was ready for a change. I got hired at the base in the cafeteria as a bookkeeper and cashier. It was a good job. My boss, Ray and I shared the office and the only time I had to work at the register was at lunch and break times. I enjoyed the break from kids and house-work. I felt I finally had a part of my life just for me. This was ok for a while but the three kids were a handful for Mom. When Gina was seven months old, I found out I was pregnant again. I quit my job. I was not happy about this baby. I thought, "I will be pregnant every seven months" and saw no end in sight. My mom's sister, Aunt Teresa had sixteen children. My sister, Beva began to call me "Aunt Teresa". She thought this was funny but I found it overwhelming.

After meeting Father Babb in Alaska, with both Gene and I try-ing to be good Catholics, we had decided, or at least I had de-cided, not to go against the church laws and use birth control. Natural family planning or "rhythm method", as they called it, was all the church considered right.

The only way Rhythm works, as I found out, is if the husband learns to dance to the same tune. To use it, you must have time to figure it all out and pick the right song to dance to.

Even though the doctors had basic knowledge, they were not really interested to help you. You had to figure it out for your-self. Obviously, I was not having much luck in this department. Gene was no help. He would just accept the pregnancy and work harder to take care of us all. Thank God, he was getting pro-moted each time as he became eligible. He was now a Staff Sar-gent which was a real step up as for us as money and importance goes. As a non-commissioned officer or NCO, you worked closer with the officer ranks. To be an officer required college, but the officers treated you with more respect as an NCO.

Our fourth baby was another boy, Jerry. This pregnancy and delivery went well too. His feet were normal, he was healthy. I guess my nerves were very on edge. I remember in delivery my doctor let the Flight Surgeon deliver the baby, for the experience. My doctor assisted, standing across the room and watching. When the baby was delivered, I said, "Thank God!" Tears started coming and my doctor said, "Mrs. Antoine, you are such a baby." Then my crying got uncontrollable. I think I was finally having after birth blues or going into shock. If the doctor had slapped me, I would have not been more upset. After the fact, I think he might have known I was so upset and crying would relieve the situation. I hope he was not just being mean. I cried uncontrollably for almost two hours until I was exhausted and fell asleep.

Gene was not at the hospital for the delivery. He couldn't find anyone to watch the kids. Not sure where Mom was, probably working. The nurse was sure that I was crying because Gene was not there. It had nothing to do with that but she kept trying to call Gene, just the same.

Four months after Jerry was born, I was pregnant again. This was the last straw, the one that broke the camel's back. I could not believe it. I didn't even get my usual seven months to figure all this out.

I cried and locked myself in the bedroom. I did not even want to talk to Gene. I knew he would just say, "It's ok, honey. It will be ok. We'll handle it." I did not want to hear that and I didn't want it to be ok. I wanted it to END. I was desperate. After having a good long pity party for myself, I finally resigned myself that being a mom was my place in this life. If I didn't just accept what God sent me I was only going to be miserable anyway.

The time passed and we had a beautiful little girl, Beth. I was so happy she was perfect and healthy. I carried a lot of guilt for the way I had behaved this time, knowing I was pregnant. I vowed I would never act that way again.

Around the same time Beth was born, we had to move. Our landlords had asked us to find another place after Jerry was born. We had lived in the new house only a couple of months when we were notified that we would get base housing. We were thrilled. It was a four-bedroom apartment that we certainly needed now. This time, we were even eligible for the Air Force to move us. They came in, packed and unpacked everything for us at the new place. It was great to have room for everyone at last.

We no sooner moved and were settled before Gene was given orders to go to France. We could not go with him because the U.S. and the French government under President De Gaul were having problems and France was closed to dependent travel. This meant I would have to be alone with the five kids. Gene went to the commander and begged to get out of the orders because it would be a hardship leaving me with a new baby and four small kids. The commander pulled some strings and Gene did not have to go to France. Whew!

We were so happy until two months later. Gene had orders again. This time to Thule, Greenland. It was another isolated assignment. No dependents. Gene tried again to get out of these orders but to no avail. He had to go. I could not stay in base housing without him being stationed there. We had to move again.

We decided that Mom and I would be better off with family around to help me. Mom wanted to go home to Missouri too. So. "Missouri, I Hear You Calling Me" became our travel song again for this move.

Missouri, I hear you calling me.

Missouri, why can't you let me be?

My heart will yearn, till I return,

Missouri's calling me.

❈ ❈ ❈

CHAPTER EIGHT- ST. LOUIS, MO-1962-63

(**D**igression)

This morning I thought about how the radio was to our generation as the I-phones are to this one.

I see everyone glued to this electronic device that doesn't even need a connection that you can see or feel sort of like the power of God.

Do you suppose God is electricity?

I guess since Ben Franklin discovered electricity and Edison lit up that first light bulb, which, by the way, is the symbol for every idea since then, the world became connected. Electricity has been our connection to each other and the whole world.

Radio: With electricity and the radio, for the first time everyone could have music without waiting for the musician to be there. With just a turn of the knob, whatever kind of music you wanted you could have. The world was now at the ends of your fingers.

Even if you didn't have electricity in your house, there were battery operated radios. The early radios were called crystal sets and had ear buds to listen to them. I remember my cousin making one for us to listen to the "Lone Ranger" back in the '40s.

The most important thing, though, was the music which communicated the way we you felt and lived.

The first thing we did in the morning was turn on the radio and the last thing before going to bed was to turn it off. Some never turned it off. Music went with us in the car. We learned all the words to every songs we liked because we heard the same songs over and over. Of course, with the invention of the phonograph and records, this became much easier. We could stop and start the record and write down the words. We didn't have to buy the sheet music anymore or listen to the older generation teach us their songs. Music was our generation and the old.

Listening to music and singing the songs of our generation were, for us, the total entertainment package. It was almost free if you could afford a radio and radios were very cheap to buy.

Sometimes people would just give them away as they were able to buy new ones. Even as poor as we were, there were very few times we didn't own a radio or knew someone that did.

As we moved from place to place, singing songs was always something we did in the car.

We either sang with the radio or without it. Music made everything seem so much better. It painted pictures in your minds of places you could see or people you could be with. If you were missing home, or mom or someone you loved or your friends, music could take you there. It connected you to the past or took you into the future or even out of this world. In my mind, music is another of God's gifts that make life here bearable.

I remember when I was about nine or ten, rain would make me feel sad. I would think of all the saddest songs and as I sang them I would cry and become even sadder. Was that depression? I loved walking in the warm summer rains and singing sad songs and crying. A little self-pity never hurts. Of course, this mood would change with the weather. I was never sad when the sun shone. The music would change to fun and happy songs then.

Someone has written a song for every emotion a person feels. What is amazing to me is there is no end to the words and different ways to put all these emotions to music.

Music has always been a big part of my life as it was Gene's. Our favorite song to sing together was "Only Make Believe". I guess it became our love song.

"Only Make Believe"

Only make believe, I love you, only make believe, that you love me.

*Others find peace of mind, in believing, Couldn't
I, couldn't you? , couldn't we*

Make believe our lips are blending, in a fathom kiss, or two or three.

Only make believe, I love you, for to tell the truth, I do.

(Left to right) Jim, Gene, Gina, Vicky, Jo Ann, Jerry

The time came to pack and leave Montana. We were on the road again. The car we thought was so big when we left St. Louis to go to Montana was now too small and cramped with the four kids, all under five, in the back seat. Gene, Mom, me, and the new baby rode in the front seat. It was almost miserable. Mom and I shuffled the baby between us. Even though I could now help Gene drive, he was not going to trade places with me. He'd rather drive. Most of the trip, I was handing the baby to Mom so I could reach over the seat, to reach the kid in the back causing trouble. It was the usual trip with kids. "Mom, he's touching me." If they were coloring, someone wouldn't share the blue. "I need it to color my rainbow."

We had to stop often because someone couldn't go pee when we stopped the last time and now needed to go. It became a game for the one being potty trained, Jerry. He had to pee every time the car stopped for gas, just to play in the water, washing his hands.

We had decided that we were going to enjoy this trip and stop and see things on our way. We finally had the time and enough money to enjoy the trip. The first day after stopping in a restaurant for breakfast and having Jerry throw up his oatmeal on the table, we decided restaurants were not such a good idea.

So, we got little boxes of cereal that could be used as a bowl for breakfast after that. We would stop in a small town, find a grocery store and ask where the nearest park was. The kids enjoyed the trip. They got to swing and slide to their hearts' content. We did this for every meal. Of course, Beth was no different from the rest of our babies who all threw up everything they ate until they were nine months old. The perfume of my day was smelling like puke. Funny how you can get used to some of these smells. I thought all moms and babies smelled that way.

Thank god, we finally had enough money for a motel now so I could wash some of the clothes. Even if we had to share the two double beds with kids, Mom got one bed and we got the other. Since they were all small, this was not a problem. Mom wasn't much bigger than Vicky was at five years old.

We made it to Yellowstone Park just as Old Faithful was burping the last of its eruptions. A lot of other smaller geysers were shooting up steam, and hot water. If we hadn't so many little ones to keep an eye on, it would have been a little more enjoyable to watch. There aren't too many places in this world where steam and hot water come spouting up out of the ground. If it weren't for the pictures of us there, I don't have any vivid memories of it. The kids were more thrilled by the buffalos we passed on the side of the road. Not sure if we made any other side trips or not. Gene would try to sleep when we stopped to eat. Finally, we got to St. Louis.

St Louis — 1962

We had to stay with Gene's mom this trip, until we could find a place of our own. Mom went to Sally and Don's. They had three little boys by this time. Poor Mom, she got no rest either. She wanted to be with them and get to know them. She had seen only Donnie, the oldest, when Sally had come to Montana. But after coming cross country with our five, I am sure she wanted to leave family behind and find a quiet place to rest.

The time at Lou and Art's was miserable for all of us. They had a three-room flat. They also had two cocker spaniels that shed a ball of hair every day. Gene and I had a roll-a-way bed and had to make pallets on the floor for the kids. This was really hard with a new baby. The first thing I did was clean the floors. This made Lou feel like I thought her house was not clean enough for me, but I could not put my kids on it to sleep, if I hadn't swept and mopped it. Their place was fine for her, Art, and the dogs but not when we brought our five kids into it. I was thankful they let us stay and know how hard this was on them too. Sometimes you just have no choices in this life.

Gene and I looked every day for an apartment for us to rent. We had less than twenty days now until he had to leave. We never thought it would be this difficult. At first, we looked for what we wanted but, as time went on, we realized we would have to settle for any place that would accept five kids. Even if we had money and could afford the rent, I was reliving my mom's life when we were forced to move to the park.

(see Chapter Two for Mom's poem, "No Children Allowed" by Betty Bainter).

Lou would have asked her tenants to move but they had kids too and really could not afford to move.

I was afraid to live upstairs with all our little ones for fear they would fall down the stairs. We finally ran out of time. We went to the Red Cross with our problem to see if Gene could get his leave extended as a hardship. The Red Cross, luckily, found us an apartment in low-income housing.

Since this housing was usually in bad neighborhoods, and sometimes with people that were a little scary, I was reluctant to go there but we did. It was not bad or in a bad area. We grabbed it and were finally settled when Gene had to leave us. It had three bedrooms so Mom came to stay with me. It did have stairs but they were inside and not as steep as the ones at Lou's. When Gene left, I had a new song to sing.

"The Saint Louis Blues".

I hate to see the ev'nin' sun go down

I hate to see the ev'nin' sun go down,

Cause my baby, he done left this town

Feelin' tomorrow like I feel today

Feelin; tomorrow like I feel today,

I'll pack my trunk and make my getaway

I got the St. Louis Blues, just as blue as I can be

That man got a heart like a rock cast in the sea,

Or else he wouldn't have gone so far from me

I love that man like a schoolboy loves his pie

Like a Kentucky Colonel loves his mint and rye

I'll love my baby till the day I die.

The days were easy to get through because I had the kids. There wasn't a minute that I didn't have things to do. When Gene would call and start feeling sorry for himself, being away from us, I would think how I would love to change places with him for even a day.

After the kids were bathed and in bed, I would finally have time to miss him. It was at bath times I missed him most. He had always bathed the kids and got them ready for bed while I fixed dinner. I was thankful that at least Vicky and Jim had gotten old enough to help me. Vicky would bathe Gina and Jim would bathe Jerry. Mom usually would go upstairs with them until they fell asleep.

I would put on our favorite songs and sit down to write to Gene. I wrote every night. The song "Love Letters" was popular again. This became our song of the times. It was sort of funny to me because years before I had seen an old war movie with Joseph Cotton, who I fell in love with. The song, "Love Letters", was the theme song for that old movie. Probably the name of the movie too. I was probably about twelve when I saw it and remembered it now again.

Even though I wrote to Gene every night, sometimes the mail would not get to Thule for days. Gene would worry so much if he didn't get a letter each time the plane came in. The letters were all he lived for besides coming home to us. I could expect a phone call when the mail was slow. Then he would get ten letters at a time and be elated. I bought a small tape recorder so the kids could talk to him and so he could hear their voices. The phone calls were so expensive and time so precious that the kids hardly got to say much more than, "Hi, Daddy," on the phone. Most of the time he would call when they were in bed so we wouldn't be interrupted. I sent him home movies but they didn't have sound on the old 8mm. He was going to get to come home for Christmas for a month. That was all we looked forward to. That and finding out where we would be going from here.

The place was intimidating to me at first. I had never been alone without Gene there. The people on one side of me had an old man who was senile. We had little back fenced-in yards about 6x6 square feet.

The old man would stand out in his yard and yell things like, "Get some help over here. These people are hungry over here!" Having never been around my own grandparents or other older people, I didn't understand what was wrong with him. He scared me with his ravings. I thought he must have been in a war. Later I found out he was a retired police officer. He would go out front every now and then and, since all the apartments looked alike, he would go in any door that was open. One day he came into our apartment.

Our kitchens had two doorways, one was right by the front door. You could go into the dining and living room and back to the entry. I was in the kitchen when he came in and he walked into the dining and living room. I didn't know what he would do. Beth was in the playpen. She was about six months old then.

I quickly ran next door to get his wife to come get him. All he did was pick up all my throw rugs and put them on the couch. She assured me he was harmless and wouldn't hurt the baby. I felt better about him after that.

On the other side of our apartment lived a retired school teacher and her husband. They argued all the time. Several times, the police would show up and talk to them. I just hoped they never decided to shoot each other and cause a bullet to come through my bedroom wall. After meeting all the people that lived around me and making friends with one couple up the street, I became less fearful and would even let my three older kids go out front to play with the other kids.

We had no air conditioning so the adults would sit out front of the apartments in the evenings when it cooled off and talk after their kids were in bed. Mom wasn't very sociable. She would watch the kids and TV while I visited.

Every day, we had a new experience with the kids. One day, Gina came crying to me when she had put a crayon up her nose and couldn't get it out. I tried but decided I had to take her to a doctor. With Mom there to watch the others, I loaded Gina in the car and off we went. Our car, the '58 Ford had trouble idling. The engine would just die in the middle of traffic. As I turned a corner, it started to die and I stepped down on the gas to keep it going. It caught hold and responded by spinning around into the other lane of traffic, scaring me and the irate lady that almost ran into me. We were all ok so I went on. At the emergency room, they were able to insert a surgical type instrument in Gina's nose and removed the crayon. I remembered the lyrics "My mother said not to put beans in your nose, beans in our nose, beans in our nose".

A few days later, Jim, who still had one foot in the cast, somehow, caught the only toe that stuck out of the cast on a drain pipe and nearly cutting his toe off. Back to the ER, for stitches and a new cast.

One day when the kids were playing and riding their bikes out front, Vicky ran her bike into a neighbor's car. The other kids threatened to tell on her. She got scared and hid from me. I hunted and called for her for over an hour, even checking the house but she was nowhere to be found. Finally, I came into the house frantic and told my mom I was calling the police. Vicky heard me and came out of the bedroom. I am still not sure where she was hiding. I had looked all over but I probably did not look under her bed. I wanted to spank her but was so glad she was safe that I didn't. At least I don't have a memory of that.

Gina again stuck a bean up her nose. This time it was a bean. I called the ER, telling them I was bringing her in. I got her dressed and, as we were ready to walk out the door, she asked me if she could blow her nose. I told her yes and out came the bean. I wonder why it had never even occurred to me to have her blow her nose.

Another major incident, again involving Gina; she had been playing out front and one of the older boys decided to put her on his bike, riding double. She somehow got her foot in the spokes and it cut her heel to the bone. He got scared and sat her off on the ground and left her. She was almost four at this time.

A lady heard her crying and brought her home to me. Again, we were off to the hospital. She had fourteen stitches in her heel. They had to stitch it inside and out. We were so lucky she hadn't bled to death.

As if this was not enough for the first six months, the second six months were no better. Gene did get home for that Christmas and that was heaven until he had to leave us and go back. I didn't know if I could do another six months without his help. Shortly after, he left. This time, I decided on a Sunday after church to drive out to my old friend Wanda's house in Creve Coeur and show the kids the one-room school we had graduated from; also, the old cabin where we had lived in Creve Coeur. I only took the three older kids.

We went to church and headed out for our adventure. This one turned out to be the worst one of that year.

It went really well until we started home. I heard a noise in the rear passenger wheel and figured I had somehow gotten a rock in the hub cap or a lug nut had fallen off. I pulled into the local filling station down the street where I had been buying my gas. I asked the attendant if he would see if he could idle my car's engine so it wouldn't keep dying. With the engine running, I told him about the noise I had heard in the wheel. I stepped out of the car to watch what he was doing. Dumb! I have to mention here that I had Gina, age four, in the front seat by me. The attendant and I walked to the back of the car, still running. I showed him which wheel, and, as he knelt to pull off the hub cap, the car started to move.

Gina had pulled the car into gear and it started across the parking lot. I ran as fast as I could to try to get into it before it got away, but it ran into another car in the lot, wrecking both cars. I was so upset about my being so stupid. I was thinking about how I was ever going to tell Gene about his car. I even forgot to see if the kids were hurt. They were crying but they looked ok. While I was on the phone to the insurance company, someone asked if the kids were ok. It finally hit me that they could have been hurt badly. Thank god, they were not. We all walked home, leaving the car for the insurance company to get fixed. At least there were no tickets to pay. But I knew, before Gene got off that plane and saw the kids, I had to tell him about this because they would never forget it.

Another problem that year with the kids; they all got chicken pox. Four of them weren't very sick but Jerry didn't seem to be getting over it as the others had. I called the clinic but they didn't seem to be concerned. Because it was a contagious disease, they didn't want me to bring him in. It worried me so I finally took him in to the hospital. He had gotten pneumonia with the chicken pox and I had nursed him through the worst of it. He could have died from it. I learned that a mother's instinct is to be listened to. She knows her child better than any doctor.

Mom had gotten a job. She wasn't sure she was going to go with us on our next move. I didn't blame her at all.

If I had other options after this year, I think I would have grabbed at them too.

One morning, as had become a habit for me, I let the kids go downstairs and turn on the tv to watch cartoons or Romper Room, a local tv program. I had warned them not to go outside or open the door to anyone. I tried to sleep in but kept with one eye open. All of a sudden, I was aware of someone standing by the bed. I opened both eyes to see a bearded man that looked somewhat familiar.

I wasn't sure who he was or how he had gotten into my bedroom. He spoke and I realized it was my brother Bill that I had not seen for over eight years. I saw him last in the Marine Corp brig at Camp Elliot, California. I thought he was working in Utah.

I was so happy to see him but immediately was aware the kids had not listened to me and let him in. He could have been any unwanted stranger. We went downstairs and I sat the kids down to lecture them about opening the door to strangers. Jim, said he was no stranger. He said, "I am your Uncle Bill. Open the dam door." So Jim did. I suppose Jim had heard me mention he had an Uncle Bill, at some point, even though he never saw him.

Bill introduced us all to his wife, Aunt Anna, whom none of us had ever met. We loved her instantly. I could hardly wait to surprise Mom with their being here. Bill had gotten out of the Marines, not because he really wanted to but the Marines thought it was a good idea. He had stayed in California and met Anna and her family. After they were married, he worked in construction and they had wound up in Utah. When that job ended, Bill wanted to come home and see mom. They took what little money and belongings they had, which included a mama cat and several kittens, and started to Missouri. Somewhere along the way, the mama cat got lost so Anna had hand fed the kittens, giving them milk in their mouths with a medicine dropper, all the way. The kids were delighted to have the kittens. We had not gotten any pets up till now. I figured I had all I could do to handle the five kids.

Mom was, of course, in Heaven to have Bill back home near us. They weren't sure how long they would stay. They both got jobs and an apartment with Mom before I left Missouri. This nightmare was about to end. Gene got his orders and we would leave in May, 1963 for Patrick AFB, Coco Beach, Florida. Finally, we were where the sun shined and no more snow. When I picked Gene up from the airport and, after the first kiss hello, I told him about the car and the rest of the story. He thought I should have told him sooner but was so happy to have this year behind us. It really didn't matter because everyone and everything was OK. The packers came and we packed the car, still with four kids in the back seat. Vicky was now allowed to sit up front, which made her very happy. I was still reaching over the seat to swat the ones that were misbehaving, but by now they were used to traveling in the car and all were potty trained except Beth. It was a much nicer move. Our song now, by Dave Dudley," was "Six Days On The Road."

* * *

CHAPTER NINE- PATRICK AFB, COCOA BEACH, FLA. 1063-65

We arrived in Florida and, after once again going to the housing office, we quickly found a nice house we could afford. Our household goods had not arrived so all we had to survive with was a kit with a few dishes and some bedding. We didn't have money for a motel, so we slept on the floor and made do.

A few days later at about 5:00 p.m. the truck arrived. With only one guy to unload everything. Gene and I were really upset with this moving company. The driver ran out of money on his way to deliver our things and had to wait for gas money from his company. He had to let his helper go. Gene and I helped to unload the truck just so we could get it done. Of course, we reported all this to the housing officer.

We got settled in and put our name on the base housing list. The town we lived in was about ten miles from the base. We were eligible now for housing but still had to wait for it. After a couple of months, we had our quarters, as they called them. It was four big bedrooms we finally had bedrooms for everyone. The school was on base and just two blocks away. Vicky had just started kindergarten in St. Louis and Jim was now old enough for kindergarten. This was great. They would be on base and could walk, as, there was hardly any traffic at the time they went to school.

Every adult probably remembers where they were on November 22, 1963. This was the blackest day America had since the assassination of President Abraham Lincoln. Our President, John F. Kennedy was assassinated by some nut named Harvey Oswald. President Kennedy was young, handsome and everyone thought he was the best thing that had happened to American politics. His wife Jackie was idolized by all. She looked like a model. Many women started trying to dress like her. The Kennedys had just had their second child, a little boy they called John-John. They had an older girl Caroline. They appeared to America and the world to be perfect. Too bad that many years later the Kennedy image would be so tarnished that Americans would never be deceived again into thinking any leader was perfect. We lost a lot of pride and respect for our leaders. I was with the kids when I heard the news. The nation mourned for a long time after this.

Life for us went on pretty much the same. Gene worked five days a week at the base and worked almost every night doing body work on cars for extra money. He and another Airman rented a small garage to work in. Florida was a haven for auto body repair because the salt from the ocean seemed to eat anything metal. Our car rusted out so bad, one day Gene took the floor mat out of the trunk to clean it and found that all the body mounts that hold the body on the frame had been eaten away. We could have taken a corner too fast and the body would not have made the corner. He fixed it so we could trade it in on a new car. Ford had just started making small passenger vans in 1965. We bought a brand new 1965 Ford Falcon van. We finally had room for all of us to be comfortable.

After we left St. Louis, Anna received word that her dad was very sick. She and Bill were going back to California to be close to her family.

Mom was diagnosed with emphysema. She was having a hard time working. We found out we could claim take her as a dependent and get the medical care she needed. She was only fifty years old and not yet eligible for Social Security. We convinced her to come live with us again.

Life was good in Florida. When Gene had time, he took the kids fishing, which Jim especially loved. Jerry was still too little but both boys found a love for fishing as they grew up. My mom had always loved to fish too. Some days she would walk over to the Ocean and try to fish. I don't remember her ever catching anything. I worried she would catch something big and it would take her out to sea like in the movie Moby Dick. She only weighed ninety-eight pounds. Sometimes we all went on the fishing trips and picnicked. We spent lots of time at the beaches.

I became more interested in the Catholic Faith and got involved at the Chapel on base. I joined the Catholic Women's Group. We made many friends, mostly the families of the guys Gene worked with and other families whose kids played with ours.

Many of the younger Airmen, seventeen to twenty-year-olds, would come to our house on the weekends to play cards and visit. Gene and I were older, twenty-five to twenty-six. The guys loved the kids and feeling part of a normal family life. We practically adopted one Airman named Keith Shields.

One of Mom's sisters, Teresa lived a couple of hours away in the Orlando area. She still had twelve kids at home. We could visit them. We had not seen them for many years.

We also had company from home. Gene's brother, Jerry and his wife Jean wanted to vacation in Florida, so they came while we were there. Having family visit us was not something we had very often. We were always able to go home on our thirty-day day leaves so that was usually the only time we saw our families. Most didn't make enough money to take vacations.

I think the only accidents we had here was when Beth, at age three going on four, overturned her tricycle and knocked out two of her front teeth. Also, Jim got a catfish barb in his leg when he caught a fish.

Our base was about ten miles from Cape Canaveral, which

would later be changed to Cape Kennedy. I think the name has now been changed back to Cape Canaveral. It was so exciting to be able to watch all the Missiles launched from the Cape and being sent to the moon and outer space. We could watch all the preliminary lift-offs on tv then go out our front door and watch it after the launch, soaring through the sky. We were a part of world history as it unfolded. The Cape was not open to the public then so we never got to go there. Everything was top secret.

One day I was watching the local tv station. They were broadcasting the countdown on a launch from the Cape. Suddenly, every Military police car on the Cape were emerging with their sirens and lights going. They surrounded two college students. It was like watching a movie. These two had left all their clothes and identification on the bank of the lagoon. They swam through the lagoon over to the site where the launch pad was. The tv cameras showed them on the screen. They were so lucky they had not been shot with the whole world watching. They did get jail time and a very heavy fine for this. Shutting down that launch cost our government millions of dollars. Afterwards, we were told that when the earth shakes from the blast off and noise, snakes and alligators are everywhere. These two were very lucky that those cameras saw them.

We got new orders at the end of 1965. We were being transferred to Hahn AFB, Germany. We would all be able to go with Gene. Even Mom decided she would go because it was the only way she could continue her medical care. She was doing ok but there was no cure for the lung problems she had and would continue to get worse. We would have to leave from McGuire AFB, New Jersey on December 8th, 1965.

After having our household goods packed and deciding what we would take to Germany, which wasn't much, we packed the van and took our leave. We went to Missouri first so Mom could visit with Beva, Sally and their families. We wanted to see Gene's mom and family too.

After a couple of weeks there, we headed for McGuire AFB to ship our car and take the plane to Germany. We spent one night at the base, then got up and went to church before heading for the plane.

December 8th is a Catholic Holy Day, the Feast of the Immaculate Conception of Mary. Flying was a new experience for Mom and the kids. They had never flown before. Vicky and Jim had been so young when we flew from Alaska, they didn't remember that. They were all excited. Mom was just fearful, I think. She had never expected to ever fly on an airplane or leave the United States. She probably did not really want to go so far from family. She was a real trouper in life and accepted whatever came her way. Once on our way, we all settled down. It was a long flight. I think it was over seven hours.

* * *

CHAPTER TEN-ARRIVING HAHN
AFB, GERMANY-1966-69

A t last we were unloading at Wiesbaden AFB, Germany. We gathered kids and luggage and headed for a bus that was waiting to drive us two hours away to Hahn AFB.

Everyone got loaded and, as we pulled out of the gate, our bus got into an accident. It was like watching an old movie. The sirens on the police cars were not the sounds of sirens in the states. They were the kind you hear in the movies of Europe.

After filling out the reports, the driver said it was too late to start out and we would have to spend the night at Wiesbaden. We were all given rooms at billeting. Billeting is the name of the temporary quarters on base, base hotels. I was happy about this, as, after that seven hour flight, I just wanted a place to relax.

In the morning, we boarded another bus without incident. We made the two hour trip to Hahn AFB. We checked in at the hotel outside the base. We had to stay there until Gene reported in and could meet with our sponsor who would help us get an apartment and get settled. The time at the gasthaus (hotel) was not enjoyable. It was a very old building with no place for the kids to play except in the room. We were expected to keep them as quiet as we could so they wouldn't bother other guests. Everything was expensive. A cup of the worst coffee (espresso) cost forty-five cents. Coffee was twenty-five cents stateside.

The bathroom was shared. This is not fun with five kids. On one trip to the bathroom, Beth, who was only four, sat down on the wooden seat and it broke. The landlady wanted us to replace it. I argued with her that it must have already been cracked, so she let it go.

After a couple of days, Gene found us an apartment. It was in a town about fifteen miles from the base called Blankenrath. The apartment was upstairs over a furniture store, not at all modern. We actually had to build a fire in the water heater in the bathroom to take a bath or do laundry. It did, however, come furnished. The kitchen had a table and six chairs. Above the sink was a small electric water heater that you had to plug in to heat water to do the dishes. I had never seen anything like this before. In the living room, there was an old lounge-type couch and a couple of mismatched chairs. The curtains were panels of black and red with surprising big yellow dots. There were two different patterns of linoleums on the floor. The bedrooms were on the third level. The beds were ok but also older. There was only one entrance, which worried me for fire reasons. Outside the apartment, there was a concrete patio with a clothes line and, although it did have a railing around it, a small child could fit between the rails. This meant the kids had to stay inside unless Mom or I went out with them. We were told we could look for something else later, but for now, this would have to do. Our moving to the base wasn't likely, since the top three ranks had first line privileges. We settled in.

Gene had to go all the way to Bremerhaven in Northern Germany close to Berlin by train to get our van. It arrived about a month later by ship. He decided to take Jim on the train with him. He told us how disgusting it was when they finally got the van. Evidently, someone had stowed away in the van, even using the bathroom in it. Someone had stolen the radio out of it too. They had to clean it all up before they could even drive it. This van was practically brand new, so that made Gene even madder. There was nothing he could do. At least it still ran all right and he didn't have to rely on someone else to get to work.

I got the kids enrolled in school. They had to ride a bus from the town to the base. All of them went but Beth. I enrolled Beth in the German kindergarten in town so she wouldn't be so bored by herself. I would have to walk her there and go get her at noon. Mom seemed ok and didn't complain much. She was a big help with keeping up with the laundry, etc. I had not had to use a wringer-washer since leaving Alaska. It took all day to do laundry this way with the large family we had.

We had clothes hanging everywhere inside the apartment. It was winter and, even if the sun was out, the clothes would just freeze on the outside line. The weather here was almost like Alaska, bitter cold. They had a cold spell that year and the fog actually froze. People all over Europe came to see it.

I had seen icicles many times, but fog was so different. It was truly a winter wonderland. Mom and I were pretty much housebound that winter. Gene had to have the car and it was too cold for her to walk anywhere. We spent most of the day in front of our kitchen window, watching whatever traffic there was and whoever was brave enough to go out in it. The Germans didn't seem to mind the weather. You would see them all bundled up and walking to the bakery in town for bread. They didn't use bags like we did. They would just stick the bare loaf of bread under their arms. I thought this was terrible because the few Germans I had met all smelled like "b.o." I was told at that time they didn't use deodorants. Most wore wool and once the smell was into the wool sweaters, it stayed.

The houses that had animals like chickens and cows all had the barns built onto the houses. This was so they could care for the animals and milk the cows if the weather turned really bad. If you ever go to the New England states, there you will still see houses like this. They mucked out their barns and piled it on the streets. The heat and steam could be seen coming off the piles. I guess the chickens liked the warmth. They always seemed to be walking on it.   The honey wagons (tractors pulling tanks) would come and collect the waste from the septic systems and streets and take it out to put on the fields. The odor took some getting used to.   The farmers didn't live on their farmland. Land was very precious and every inch was used to grow their crops. One thing we were told about Germany was not to be offended if we passed a German man peeing on the side of the roads. Bathrooms were not common in this part of Germany. One day, when the farmer across the street was butchering a hog right in front of his house, Mom and I sat at the window and watched. He had some other men helping him. All of a sudden, Mom was closing the outside shutter because one of them decided he had to go pee. He looked up at her and smiled. She was offended big time!

I guess the realization that Germany was so small a country and is only about the size of our state of Montana was my biggest surprise. Since Hitler had been so powerful, seizing other nearby countries, I and most Americans thought Germany was the size of the U.S. Now, I wondered how Hitler had ever become a threat to the whole world. It made no sense to me once I had lived here. It made no sense, either, because the people were very religious. In all the fields in this area, you would see in one corner a small shrine to the Virgin Mary or a cross.

Most everyone went to the church, which was very old, built before World War II. I am still not sure these farmers even knew there was a war. They still had very few ways to get around, mostly on foot, on bicycles or on their tractors. You would see three or four ladies, fifty years or older coming to church on Sunday morning, riding on a tractor together.

Most of the older people were very friendly and would speak to us. Most could speak some English.

The younger teenagers were not as friendly. It was harder for the kids to make friends. One day, when I let the three older kids walk to the store alone, a group of German boys chased them and cornered Jim in a lumber yard. The girls ran home to get me. When I got there, they backed off and I got Jim and went home. The more I thought about it, the madder I got. I knew this would keep happening if I didn't do something. I went to the local policeman and told him what had happened. He went with me to find those boys.

When we found them, he gave them a good talking to in English. When I had tried to talk to them, they just laughed and kept saying, "Nicht verstehen American." I realize now that they all spoke English and understood. They were just being brats. We never had trouble after that. Jim made friends with one boy, Hans Peter, who lived at the edge of town, very nice family. Gina made a good friend also, Kristianna.

Jim 1967 Germany

They all learned something from each other. Mostly that people are the same where ever they come from.

Mom hardly went out except when we would go to the base to the doctors or shopping. She was fighting depression and the doctors had given her Valium. This was the medicine of the day. It seemed everyone I knew who was not happy in Germany was on Valium. I had met women who were leaders in the chapel programs and ladies' groups who began to walk and function like zombies. All were on Valium.

One day I walked into the room where Mom was using the wringer washer. She had run her hand into the wringer and was crying, trying to pull it free. All she had to do was hit the lever to turn it off but she couldn't think that clearly. I got her hand free but and it was mangled. The school bus was coming down the street so I got on it. I rode to some officer's house and begged his wife to drive Mom and me to the base. I had to leave the kids alone at the house. We got to the base and I called Gene. He drove us back home. I had very little knowledge of medicines in those days. I don't think the doctors had much, either. As time went on, Mom became so depressed we had to take her to the mental hospital for treatment. This scared her and she quit taking the medicine. She got better but the doctors decided that we would do better if we lived on the base, so we got a medical permit to get base housing.

Before we moved from Blankenrath in the Spring, there was what they called a Kermis or carnival. It was like the Mardi Gras in New Orleans. There were booths and a big tent set up for a beer garden and dance. We took the kids during the day. One German man followed us from booth to booth, watching the kids. Germans didn't have big families. After the kids went to bed, Gene and I went back to the dance. This was the first dancing we had done for a long time. It was a great time. When we came into the tent, the German man, who had watched us with the kids stood up and said, "Ah, zee mama." We met and sat with three couples from Amsterdam. Only one man, Otto Kasstenar, could speak any English. He translated whatever we said to the others. He told us what they said. One of the men would all of a sudden say, "Money in the pocket" or "A dog in the box. That's good English!" and we would all laugh. These three older men were the best dancers I had ever danced with. They could waltz and polka, I danced all night. Gene would dance with their wives. This was the most fun I had had in years. I hated for it to end. The Kasstenars invited us to come to Amsterdam when their holiday was over. We went to see them before we left Germany. We wrote letters occasionally for some years after that but finally lost contact with them.

We finally got base housing and Mom seemed to do so much better. We had really good neighbors, the Kirkpatricks, Peggy and Sam and their three girls. Peggy was German from the Frankfurt area and had come to the states to Texas. Sam was a tall, skinny Texan. We are still friends today, almost fifty years later. They live in Abilene, Texas. Our doorways opened into the same stairwell, so it was like living together. The kids could go back and forth and play with each other. We would spend the weekends after church going to the NCO club for lunch. The club played what they called "Kiddie Bingo" on Sundays for prizes. Afterwards, the different bands would play music for the kids for an hour or so. They let the kids come on stage and sing. All the kids loved this. Beth, our five-year-old, was especially talented. One band leader from England, Val Merrill liked her so much he would feature her.

She had learned all the old songs from Mom and me from the '40s and '50s. Since our radio was stolen from the van, we made our own entertainment, singing everywhere we went. Beth's being able to remember songs so well was an added blessing for us. Mom, who had always used her poems and writing all her life to express herself, started to write songs again. She wrote a new song almost every week and would teach it to Beth. We all loved spending our time at the club.

I joined the Catholic Women's Group and got to know the Chaplain, Father Whalen. He had brought his mom to Germany too. I started taking Mom and Mrs. Whalen to Bingo every week. They both loved to gamble. There were slot machines at the club. Mrs. Whalen liked the NCO club because Father Whalen had to go to the Officer's club and everyone knew them there. Some would tease her about her gambling. Here, no one would say anything, even if they recognized her, since she belonged to the officers' ranks. Mom and Mrs. Whalen became friends and finally had someone their own ages to talk to. One day at the club, Gene put a nickel in a machine that a guy had just finished playing and hit the jackpot. The guy who had been playing it introduced himself. He was Bill McKee. The McKees had just gotten to Germany too. Bill introduced us to his wife Zita. Zita was of German descent but was an American German from North Dakota. They had five children too, one boy and four girls. We met at mass on Sundays, then went to the NCO club. We became fast friends.

We would spend almost all our free time together after that meeting. We were still living in Blankenrath when we first met Bill and Zita. They were living in a German village, Hecken. They lived above a gasthaus, a bar and restaurant. The first New Year's we were there, they invited us to a party at the gasthaus. We had not gone out for New Year's Eve since we had lived in Montana. I knew Gene would drink some so we had planned to stay overnight at their house. I never liked to be driving on New Year's Eve. There were a lot of Germans that worked on the base there too. Everyone was drinking but me, I guess. The Americans were furnishing the Germans American whiskey and the Germans were feeding the Americans schnapps. The schnapps, of course, was much stronger than the whiskey the Americans were used to. At least, it was stronger than what Gene usually drank. Even before we had our dinner, which I was looking forward to, Gene disappeared, going to the bathroom in the basement. He didn't come back for what I thought was an exceptionally long time. I sent some of the guys to check on him. They said he told them he was ok and would be there in a minute. Gene finally had someone, Palmasano help him up the stairs. Of course, by now I am getting angry and I wanted to go home. He didn't want me to drive so he layed down in the van for a little while. It was freezing out and when I saw he wasn't going to enjoy this party and I certainly was not, I took the keys, said our goodbyes, and drove us home. He had to almost crawl up the stairs to our apartment. I sure couldn't carry him. The next morning, he awoke and both of his eyes were pools of blood, enough that it scared us. I drove him to the base to the doctor. The doctor decided that an antibiotic he had taken and the alcohol he drank could have been the problem. I don't think we realized how lucky we were at that time. When I think back, I often wonder if this had anything to do with his later medical problems.

Since Beth was singing at the NCO club on Sunday, I taught her to sing a parody to an old song that goes, "I want a girl, just like the girl that married dear old dad". The original parody goes, "I want a beer, just like the beer that pickled my old man...". I changed a few words s to fit the occasion.

I want some schnapps just like the schnapps

That pickled my old man

They were the schnapps and the only schnapps

That Daddy ever had

Some good old-fashioned schnapps

Made so strong

It took Popasano to carry Daddy home

I want some schnapps just like the schnapps

That pickled my old man

Gene was a little upset with me at first for teaching it to her and letting her sing it on stage, but it became an instant hit with all our friends who requested it several times after that.

It saddens me that they and Gene are gone from our lives at this writing. Our friendship lasted their whole lives. Probably Gene, Bill, and Zita are just waiting for me to play Pinochle with them.

Germany was a great assignment for us. It was like a three year holiday or vacation after moving on base. The NCO club got some of the best entertainment of our times and we saw them all, The Everly Brothers, Johnny Ray, Fats Domino, Hank Snow, Lefty Frizzle, Joni James, and so many more, plus, some of the greatest bands in Europe. It was one continuous party.

We traveled the country and went all over Europe.

Madura Dam Holland 1968

The base had a trip to Rome for eighty dollars a person for a week. Zita and Bill went with us. We rode a train through the Alps to Italy and had a hotel two blocks from St Peters. We had a general audience with Pope John the XXIII. That was a once in a life time experience but not one I would want to do again. There were so many people jammed into the area, people were getting sick and even passing out. Seeing St Peter's, the Sistine Chapel, the art, the Catacombs was like walking through history and seeing it for the first time. We had USO tours every day. We had a young friend, Larry Jankowski who was becoming a priest, studying in Rome. Larry had come to our base and gotten acquainted with us. He loved all our kids. He would play guitar and taught the kids songs. He was an American from Milwaukee. Wisconsin. When we finished our tours, Larry would come to the hotel and show us Rome at night. He took us by train on a day trip to the Mediterranean Sea.

This will always be one of the greatest thrills of my life. I had never seen water so blue and beautiful. In Rome, history comes alive. It is like being there in real time. We went to a site where chariots used to race. They put on a show called, sounds and lights. There was nothing to see but the lights, you are in total darkness. All we heard were the sounds of the chariots and the soldier's voices. Wherever we heard a voice or sounds, a light came on, and your imagination took you to the action. It is hard to explain but you felt you had been in this place and seen all that went on there; yet, we had only experienced it through the sounds and lights.

It was amazing.

Mom and a couple of airmen who worked for Gene and Bill, watched the kids for us. It was close to being in Heaven.

Ann Frank House 1968

We drove somewhere almost every weekend to see one castle after the other. We went to Belgium to see where our troops had fought the Battle of the Bulge. We spent a week in Holland going to see the Anne Frank house, Madura Dam, the tulip fields, and, of course, the Kasstenars. We went to Zurich, Switzerland on a ferry via Lake Constance (Konstanz). We heard the echo of the trumpet on the Konigsee and toured the Chapel St. Bartholomew. We camped out in the Black Forest. There, I learned not to follow a German when they go for a walk. They are just walking rapidly, not going to sight see. There was no castle up that mountain, just a two hour walking trail. We rode the boats down the Zell and Mosel rivers. We spent a week in Berchtesgaden at the Hotel General Walker, which was one of Hitler's famous resorts for his troops. The Americans used it as a recreational area after the war. We went to Austria and toured the castle, cathedral, and Von Trapp family home where "The Sound of Music" was filmed. We toured the Salt Mines in Austria. This was really a great tour. First, we were given a miner's outfit. It is all black with a beret-type cap. Then we went down into the mines, riding a small train that we sat on like a horse, down into the mines. After getting into the mine, each person was is given a piece of leather to sit on as you slide down a ninety-foot double rail into the mine. Once at the bottom, we took a short boat ride on an underground lake. The lake was made from the water used to extract the salt from the walls of the mine. After the mine tour, we went back to the hotel.

Mom was not feeling well and had a headache, so she went to the room to rest. There was a miniature golf course at the hotel so we sent the kids off to do that. Gene and I went to get a cup of coffee and relax. Before we finished our coffee, the kids were back. Jim held one tooth in his hand, telling us Gina had somehow gotten her golf club into Beth's mouth pulling out the two front teeth she had left. They could only find the one tooth. Poor Beth. She was trying so hard not to cry. They had told her we would probably have to go home if she cried. Now the tears were coming as she got to us. We took her to the base clinic. They checked her out and told us how lucky she was. They were only her baby teeth. She would eventually have lost them. There was nothing else we could do for her but watch for infection and give her Tylenol for the pain, poor baby.

That finished our vacation.

We did all this on our grocery money. I can't even imagine what a tour like this would cost today for even only one person. I had another week in Berchtesgaden at the General Walker all by myself. Gene and Mom watched the kids so I could go to a Catholic Women's Conference with Father Whalen, his mom and another woman from the base. It was the first time since I had been married that I did not have to think about anyone but myself.

I have to be honest, I was in no hurry to get back home. I was happy after I got there, though. Father Whalen and Mrs. Whalen are gone now. We stayed in touch and went to see them over these past fifty years. Father had a great cabin on Lake Katherine in Vermont.

One other important part of our time in Germany was traveling with the base softball team, the Hahn Hawks. Gene played slow pitch softball for the base team. He played first base. Each base in Germany had a team. When the games were scheduled at other bases, the team and all the families would go on the military buses to the games. Most were on weekends.

Each base was at least a two hour ride. Sometimes, to occupy the kids, they would play Bingo for prizes, sing songs, or someone would start saying, "Who stole the cookie from the cookie jar?" This might go on for a half hour or more till even the kids got tired of it. Everyone learned the cheer for the team.

We are the Hahn Hawks

The mighty mighty Hahn Haws

Everywhere we go

People want to know

Who we are

So we tell them...

This was a great group of people. The kids were all well behaved and we would meet new people and get to see other sights along the way.

Our team did win the championship one year and got the trophy to keep at our base.

An airman that had been stationed with us at Patrick AFB, Keith Shields was stationed at Sembach AFB in Germany. Keith visited us at Hahn AFB and brought another young airman into our lives, Terry Odalen.

We lost track of Keith after Germany but still hear from Terry and his family even today via email.

Christmas 1967 Blankenroth, Germany

Evelyn, the sister of my old friend Mary from Kimmswick, who had come to get Mary and me when we ran away from home, had married a man in the Air Force and was at a base called Bitberg AFB in Germany. Evelyn was almost a relative now since my sister Beva had married her brother Robert. The time finally came for us to leave Germany and it was with a sad heart we left all that behind. Our next assignment was in Tucson, Arizona, at Davis Monthan AFB. We were happy, though, to get to go home and see our families again.

* * *

CHAPTER ELEVEN-LEAVING GERMANY-1969-71 TUCSON, AZ.

LEAVING GERMANY - ARRIVING TUCSON, AZ — 1969-71

We gathered in the parking lot at the Hahn AFB NCO Club, waiting for the military buses that would take us back to Wiesbaden-Rhein-Main AFB. We were going home to the United States. All our friends were there to bid us farewell (Auf Wiedersehen). The trip home was long. We did stop in New-foundland to refuel but weren't allowed to get off the plane. I managed to get one of the crew to pick up a rock for each of the kids as souvenirs, though, I'm not sure that, with all the rocks collected in the years to come, we kept them.

We landed at McGuire AFB, New Jersey and stayed the night there. We waited at the base for Gene to go pick up our van that we had shipped back. Luckily, this time it was waiting for us and clean.

We had decided before we left Germany to try to and visit

the Corbins, who had been our friends and neighbors in Alaska. They were now stationed near the Annapolis Naval Academy a few miles from Washington D.C. Peggy and Jack were familiar with the area, so we had a great tour of the Capital, Smithsonian Museum, Tomb of the Unknown Soldier, Lincoln and Jefferson Memorials at the Tidal Basin and Rock Creek Park. We didn't tour the White House or Washington Monument but did go and look at them. We stayed four or five days with Peggy and Jack and then headed for St. Louis. We wanted to spend as much time with family as we could before going to our next base, Davis Monthan AFB in Tucson, Arizona.

We checked in at the base and were able to get temporary quarters until we found a house. It was only a couple of days before we found a duplex right near the school, Bonillas Elementary. It was only about five minutes from the base. Gene started work right away and I enrolled the kids in school. All five were in school now. Beth was in second grade and Vicky was in Junior High or Middle School.

Mom was doing ok and able to be home alone so I decided I would look for a job. Vicky was old enough now to help Mom keep an eye on the other kids after school. At first, I went to work for a temp agency, Kelly Girls.

We were now closer to Bill and Anna in San Diego and wanted to visit them. They came over to Tucson as soon as we got settled in. Mom was so happy to be able to see them again. It had been seven 7 years since we were together in St. Louis. We made a trip out to California to their place soon after their visit. While we were in Jamul, California visiting Bill and Anna, the kids got acquainted with Anna's nieces and nephews, the Reeds. They had a horse and their dog had just had a litter of puppies. Gene and the kids wanted one of the puppies. I was out numbered, so we went back to Tucson with a puppy named "The Red Baron." He, of course, was a German shepherd. We also had a guinea pig. I don't think the rat had a name. It was not coming in my house, either. When we got home, Gene and the kids made a pen in the yard for the guinea pig and built a doghouse for Red. We had a big fenced-in backyard.

Having never lived in the kind of heat they have in Arizona, we didn't think about how hot it was for the guinea pig. It died shortly after we got it from heat stroke. Red tolerated the heat. There was a tree for shade in the yard. We had never had a dog or any kind of pets before moving to Tucson.

We had to rent and that was hard enough with five kids. I didn't want to travel with dogs in the car after my little dog Timmy had gotten hit when I was a kid.

We had hoped, when we got this assignment, that we would get to stay in Tucson for two or three years. After a while, I got a job at the base as a Book Keeper-Cashier at the base service station. I had a great boss, Bud Bland, and found I really liked working with men much better than women. Everyone seemed to adjust to the new place in the beginning.

Gene still picked up a few auto body jobs for extra money. He was also picked for the base soft ball team. We went to all his games. Our boys now played little league and went to a local park for fishing every chance they had. There was another park closer to the house where all the kids in the neighborhood went. Here, I think I failed as a parent. I should have gone there and checked out that park more carefully. Unknown to me, all of my kids except Beth had started to smoke, even Jerry, who was only nine years old. Gene was still smoking in the house and so was my mom, so I didn't suspect the kids were smoking. Mom found out Vicky and Jim were and told me. Every day I was coming home to arguments because she would tell me what she had found. Of course, they would deny it. I suppose now that the reason Jim was so good about taking Jerry with him was because he let Jerry smoke so he wouldn't tell on him. Vicky was almost fourteen and arguing about everything. She resented Mom for telling on her. No one was happy any more. I am not sure what Gina was doing. She had made friends with a little girl her age across the street named Athena and spent most of her time at their house. We loved Athena. She was Mexican and so beautiful with her long black hair and dark eyes. She was so completely different from Gina, who was as beautiful but very blonde. Mom was so taken with Athena she even wrote a poem about her. We took Athena on one of our trips to Missouri and the way people looked at us was like we might have kidnapped her.

Our first Christmas in Tucson, Vicky and Jim were outside when and a parakeet landed on Vicky's head. She and Jim brought it in and asked to keep it. I figured it was someone's Christmas present so I said they could keep it until someone claimed it. We had to get a cage. No one put up "lost bird" signs or came to claim it, so they gave it a name, "Dirty Bird". For such a small creature, it made the biggest messes, throwing bird seed all over the floor. I decided, then, that a bird in the house would not be something I wanted. The kids and Gene loved this bird, Jim especially! He would take it out of the cage and talk to it. The bird did seem to say, "dirty bird" after a while. Jim would lie on the floor on his stomach near the cage with his head on his arms and the bird would walk around until it found a place to go in. Shortly after we got the bird, the lady next door, who talked to Gene all the time about her dog, found a beagle. She asked Gene if he wanted it. He did. It was a female but was named "Toby." We had a hard time keeping Toby in the yard and one day she chased a boy on a bike. She nipped him and it upset me. I don't like a dog that you have to worry about. Later, we found out Toby was going to have puppies. Now, more than ever, I wanted to give her away, but Gene and the kids wanted to keep her. She had the puppies and the puppies cried all the time. We discovered Toby had a breast infection. She couldn't feed the puppies. Gene and Mom took turns feeding them, trying to keep them alive. The puppies all died so Gene agreed to give Toby up. We took her to the pound hoping someone else would adopt her. For someone who didn't want animals to take care of, all of a sudden we had more than we needed.

Easter came and someone gave Gina a baby chicken. I let her keep it because these Easter chicks usually die. This one didn't. When I got up at night, I'd find my mom, sitting in front of the oven and feeding the chick wrapped up in a towel. They named the chick "Chirpy." Mom even wrote a story about Chirpy for Gina. Chirpy not only lived, it became a full-grown chicken. It would fly up on the roof of the house and get out of the yard and go walking down the sidewalk. We finally got tired of going after it, so we put it in the cage that was made for the guinea pig. We moved it to the shade. One day my mom calls me at work. She is upset and crying. She puts Gina on the phone to tell me what was is going on. I had envisioned all the worst things happening to one of the kids. Gina was crying too and says, "Mommy, something murdered Chirpy!." It didn't just kill it. It MURDERED it!

I thanked God that was all the phone call was about and tried to console them, all the while, thinking I am glad for one less thing to aggravate me with.

Now, all we had to deal with was the dog, Red, whom I had learned to like. He was a good dog and stayed in the yard. He didn't bite or bark a lot. We still had the parakeet, Dirty Bird. The kids were doing better with cleaning up the seeds. Life was getting routine here now.

Jim found a cat and we kept it. We still had Dirty Bird and Red. The cat had kittens and we got rid of all but one that the kids wanted to keep. One morning I got up to a crime scene in the living room. The bird cage had been knocked over. There were little drops of blood in a trail on the floor. Even a couple of little toe nails. There could only be one killer, the cat. It was time for me to make decisions about pets. The kids were so upset that Dirty Bird was gone. They really didn't object to getting rid of the cat and kitten. I also convinced them when Dad came home we would have to make that choice anyway as I was not traveling with cats. Red and five kids were enough.

My sisters both decided to visit us that summer. This was the first time we had family visit us, except for the time in Montana when Sally left Don. Beva, Robert and their girls stayed only a couple of days with us. They were on their way to Jackson Hole, Wyoming. They wanted to go white water rafting and see the Grand Canyon. It was their first real vacation.

Sally and Don now had five kids too and wanted to take them to Disneyland. They brought Don's old Aunt Beulah with them. Beulah was helping them out with the expenses too. After a short time at our house in Tucson, we all packed our cars with clothes and kids and headed for Bill and Anna's in San Diego. We planned for all of us to go to Disneyland together. With Aunt Beulah, Mom, and ten kids, we made the trip. We got as far as Gila Bend, Arizona when we needed gas. Gas was thirty-seven cents a gallon at the base in Tucson. It was forty-two cents in Gila Bend. Gene thought it would be cheaper in Yuma because there would be more stations. He decided to go on. About half way between Gila Bend and Yuma, we ran out of gas. It was about 2:00 in the afternoon in the heat of the day. Don still had gas, so the guys decided to siphon some gas from Don's car to ours. Only problem was, we had no hose to siphon with. Aunt Beulah to the rescue. She had an enema bag, brand new. She hadn't used it. She'd packed it just in case. At first Don tried, then Gene, but I guess the thought of the enema was too much. Neither could get the gas to siphon. Finally, we all decided Don would have to go on to Yuma and get gas to bring back to us. So, we found what shade we could and prayed he wouldn't get lost. He hadn't done much traveling on his own. He did well and found his way back. We were on our way again. We finally got to Bill's and, because they were on a well, we didn't want to stay long with all the kids. Bill had taken care of part of the flushing of toilets. He had built an outhouse for the kids to pee in. Anna had hung curtains and decorated it. It was cute and did the trick. The next day we went to Disneyland. We had been able to get all the tickets we needed at the base. It cost us a grand total of eighteen dollars for all of us. Each book of E-tickets cost a dollar. We stayed until they closed. Everything was perfect until we came out of "Pirates of the Caribbean". We each forgot to count heads and relied on someone else to do it. We lost Jerry, who was nine. I guess we kept walking and he didn't follow us. Finding him took two hours out of our fun time. Thank God, he went, or someone took him, to the Lost and Found. It was a very scary time for us all, especially Jerry. We never got to do that again together. We could never afford to take ten kids there again. The prices changed drastically after that.

We were in Tucson a little over a year when Gene came home with new orders. He had to go to an isolated assignment at Indian Mountain, Alaska. After talking about it, we decided I would keep my job and stay in Tucson. It was only a one year tour. He would get to come home for a month after the first six months. I was not looking forward to him leaving this time. The kids were older and should have been more help, but they were doing things now that they knew they shouldn't be doing and worrying me more.

As I look back at this time of life in the '60s, I can see that it wasn't just our kids growing up and our life that was changing. The world as we knew it had changed. While we were in Germany, the "free love and hippie movement" had started. From the news we got overseas, we expected to see hippies on every corner. All sloppily dressed, lazy and doing drugs in public. Fortunately, it was not like that at all. There were the druggie-looking young people around at the shopping centers, schools, and airports, but it hadn't taken over every young person or group of kids. The music and movies had become less moral. Now they had to put ratings on movies so that only the less moral adults could go to them.

Now, even cartoons were labeled "Adult" cartoons on tv. How funny can that be? Some kids started sniffing glue and hanging themselves to get what they called a "high". Many got so high they couldn't loosen the rope in time and they died. We think this was the cause of our friends, the McKee's, son Randy's death.

Along with this movement came "the pill". So many more young people were not afraid now of having babies. They became more immoral and sexually active with their "free love". The pill didn't stop all babies being born because it wasn't always used according to the directions, even by married couples. Babies born to unwed mothers was still a big problem. There was the attitude by many that "if it feels good, you should do it", not deprive yourself of anything you feel gives you pleasure. Even the Catholic Church went through the Vatican 2 adjustment period, examining the Church laws to see if changes should be made. During this time, most young Catholics were told, "let your conscience be your guide." Very few had a conscience. In the end, nothing changed except, you could eat meat on Friday if you did a good deed like visiting the sick. Once the door was opened and the rules relaxed, there was no going back. More and more, mothers went to work, leaving a lot of teenagers on their own.

I thought with Mom in our home this was ok for us too, but she didn't carry the authority with our kids that I had. Looking back, I think I should have stayed home a little longer with them. If I had been home, I might have seen or caught them with cigarettes and gotten to know who they were talking to at the park. I didn't want to quit my job. It was my escape from some of my responsibilities, a place where I was treated not like just a mom or wife but just a person of equal status with those around me. The time came for Gene to leave us and life went on much the same.

One day I talked my mom into having her picture taken for the family at a studio on the base. We never had a good picture of her. I made an appointment on Saturday morning to have her hair done and the picture made. The kids were at the house when we left. Jerry had a little league game and was going to go to his game. After we left the photo studio, I stopped in at the service station to call home and check on the kids. As soon as I walked into the station, the guys working told me to go straight to the hospital. Jerry was taken there by ambulance. He had gotten severely burned. I still had no idea how. Mom and I drove to the hospital. Thank God, we were already on the base. I had never seen any of my children seriously hurt, never, where I thought they might not live. This was the worst pain I had ever seen one of them in. The treatment was as painful as the injury. I had to wait until they treated him to find out how serious the burns were. Both legs at the top had serious burns and there were some smaller burns on his body. He couldn't tell us how it happened. Gina's friend, Athena's mom was a nurse and was at the hospital with him when I got there. She said she saw the flames on the porch and saw Jerry run to an ice chest of water sitting in the yard. She kept him there until the ambulance got to the house. We stayed at the hospital until he was asleep. I had called home and the other kids were there and nothing else had burnt on the house. When I got home finally, the story I got was Jerry was going to his ball game. He was on the front porch when something ignited a bleach bottle of gas. Jim had gotten the gas for the lawn mower. I still feel that if I had paid attention, that gas would not have been there. Blaming myself was not going to help me get through this.

When I could question Jerry about the gas blowing up, he told me because I was upset with them all smoking, he decided to burn up the cigarettes he had left. When he lit the match, the gas blew up. Thank God, the water was close and he had sense enough to get to it. Now, the main worry were the burns. They were so deep and near the bones, the doctors were afraid of a bone infection. This could cause blood poisoning and possible loss of his legs or maybe his life.

I called Gene and he wanted to come home, but that meant he would have to stay longer when he went back. We decided that if it looked like it would take a turn for the worse, I would go to the Red Cross and get him home.

Mom stayed with Jerry when I couldn't be there. I could never have gotten through this without her help. The other kids pitched in and kept things quiet at the house. I guess I wasn't paying much attention to any of them now, just praying Jerry would be ok.

My boss, Bud, was really good to me. He covered my job at work and even let me take the work to the hospital. When Jerry was asleep, I would get my work done. One of the Corpsmen that took care of Jerry had given him a little rubber alligator. Jerry named the alligator George. The treatment they used was a whirlpool bath. It removed the dead skin with the spinning of the water. It was still very painful. One day they took Jerry to the whirlpool while Mom was there and he began to cry and wanted "George". Mom didn't know George was the alligator. She ran back to the ward to find George. No one there was named George. The nurses didn't know who George was. Finally, the corpsman that had given the thing to Jerry got the toy and took it to him. That day was Mom's hardest day. Mine was a few days after that. I was in the room and decided to stay while they changed Jerry's dressings. I didn't make it through that. I was collapsing outside his room crying. I guess I finally had my meltdown. I was ashamed that I couldn't stay with him when he had to endure that pain every day. We got really lucky. He didn't get any infections and his legs finally healed enough for him to come home. He would have to go to physical therapy for walking but he could finally come home. At home, he stayed in bed for a while. I really don't have an exact memory of all the time this entailed. The song "Leaving on a Jet Plane" was his favorite song. It was on a tape and he played it over and over. I think it was his way of dealing with Gene being gone. He needed his dad and maybe we should have had him come home.

Gene did get home shortly after Jerry came home from the hospital. We all needed a break so Gene and I went car shopping for something more comfortable than our old Ford van. We found a 1971 big Ford station wagon, our first car with air-conditioning. We could make Jerry a bed in the back for the trip. It had a roof rack, so we tied what we could on top and took a trip to Missouri. Gene's mom and our families were all worried about Jerry too. We had a good visit and, when we returned to Tucson, Gene had to return to Indian Mountain to finish his tour of duty. He was ok now to go back since he saw Jerry was going to be all right.

We had more good news when we got back to Tucson. Gene's Commander from Alaska called him to tell him he had made Master Sergeant. He was also going to receive the Meritorious Medal for going above and beyond in doing his job. This promotion was a big deal. It was the first in the top three grades an enlisted man could make. Most of the guys we had come in the service with never made this rank. It also meant more money. The medal he was awarded was for taking the mail to the guys that were isolated at what they called Top Camp. The only way to get to this camp in the winter was by half-track dozers. Even on the tractors, this was extremely dangerous but mail to these isolated guys and most service men was more valuable than food and drink. It had always been so to Gene and he wanted to be sure they got letters from home. I think this and worrying about Jerry and all of us was going to take its toll later. He returned to Alaska, finished his tour, and got his new orders. We were moving to Rantoul, Illinois to Chanute AFB.

Chanute was one of the most important training schools in the Air Force. Gene was excited about his new assignment. He was going to be an instructor in vehicle maintenance. He was now dreaming of following in his older brother Lloryel's footsteps and becoming a teacher when he retired from the Air Force.

The time came for our move and I decided since Mom would be moving so far from Bill again, I would meet Gene in San Diego instead of Tucson. I had all our stuff packed and gave up our apartment. We still had the '65 van so the kids and I took all our Christmas ornaments and decorated the van. We were going to try to be in Missouri for Christmas. When Gene got home, we would have to come back through Tucson on our way to Missouri and we would pick up the van then. The day we left to go to San Diego, it snowed in Tucson. It was the first snow they had had in fourteen years. Bud tried to get me to stay and leave the next day because there were some mountains outside of Yuma to cross over. I didn't want to stay. We would have had to stay with someone and I knew Mom would be uncomfortable. We also had the dog Red. So, on we went in our big new station wagon. Me, my mom, five kids and the dog. A little way out of town, the wind was bad and there was a pickup truck in front of me. One of those big white buckets flew out the back of the truck and bounced once in front of our car, but luckily it veered off to the side of the road. The snow ended a short time after that and the road was clear. We settled in and enjoyed the drive.

Just before coming into Yuma, I noticed flashing lights coming up behind me. I pulled to the side of the road. It was me he was after. A very nice CHP approached the car and the kids held their breath. I am sure Mom did too. He said, "You didn't slow down for the zone change." I said," I guess the kids were being so good I was just enjoying the drive." He said, "You didn't slow down for the two before that, either." He took my license and when he returned, he gave me a warning. No ticket! I guess it was because of all the kids and the dog or just Christmas being near. I carefully drove the speed limit after that. We got to Anna and Bill's safely. Things were good. Gene was due within the next two days.

The next day Gene called me. He was really upset. He had been told he could leave early, and on his way to the plane, his leave was canceled. He told me to go to the Red Cross and tell them anything to get him home. The following day I went to the Red Cross to plead my case. I told them what I had been through with Jerry and that Bill's home was on a well with limited water so we couldn't stay any longer with him. The Red Cross guy went and talked to someone else. He came back and told me they couldn't see that I had an emergency. I went to pieces and told him that I was dropping all five of my kids off to them in the morning and I was going to Missouri by myself. They could deal with getting their father home and I left. The Red Cross called just as I got back to Bill's. They asked if Monday morning would be soon enough. This was Friday. I told them I would wait till Monday. Gene was home on Monday.

We spent a couple more days with Bill and Anna and headed back to Tucson to get the van. We hadn't gotten very far when flashing lights were coming up behind Gene this time. He was sure he wasn't speeding but this CHP was not sympathetic to him. He got a ticket. Maybe there was a record of the CHP that had stopped me in the same car. We drove on to Tucson and spent the night on the base. We had a tow bar and hooked up the van to the wagon. We let Red ride in the van. He sat in the front seat all the way. People stared at him and all the Christmas decorations hanging in the windows. It was a good trip from there to Missouri. We arrived at Sally and Don's on Christmas Eve. We went shopping for a few things after the kids went to bed. It was a great Christmas! Gene was home and we were with family.

Merry Christmas 1971.

* * *

CHAPTER TWELVE-
CHANUTE AFB 1971-75

After Christmas, Gene and I drove to Illinois to Chanute A.F.B. from Sally and Don's.

We checked into the base and found an apartment in off-base new housing called Chanute Homes. We also placed our name on the list for on-base housing, but that was going to take a while, even with Genes' new rank.

After getting our household goods delivered, we went back to Missouri for the kids and Mom. Donnie, Sally's oldest son, came with us to visit.

We didn't have a yard, so the dog, Red, had to stay inside. Donnie and Jim took Red for a walk shortly after we moved in. They were only gone a short time when Jim called, crying. Red had gotten hit by a car. The driver never stopped. The local sheriff saw them beside the road. He picked up the dog and the boys and took them to the Vet. The Vet told us it would cost about $125.00 to treat Red. We were already strapped for money, as always after a move and especially right after Christmas. I wanted to have the dog put to sleep but Gene and the kids were so upset we couldn't do it. There were no permanent injuries, so we decided to treat him. I decided there would be no more pets after Red, especially after all the problems we had with them. We just did not have the extra money for vet bills. Thank God, our kids had free medical care so I didn't have to make those choices for them. (Joking)

We had good neighbors at these apartments. The older lady next door, Judy, was from England. She took a special interest in Beth. She told me when Beth was singing in the bathroom, she (Judy) would open her medicine cabinet door so she could hear her better.

My dad was living in Indiana, about four hours away. I hadn't seen him for years. After we were settled, we took a Sunday drive to visit him and his third wife, Gertrude. He and Gertrude had married just before Gene and I were married. I had always felt I was breaking the fourth Commandment by not loving my dad. Later it was explained to me that honoring your parents didn't mean you had to love them. It meant if they were good decent people, themselves you should never bring shame to your parents by your own actions. I forgave him and others because I believed somehow they had convinced themselves that they didn't intentionally want to hurt others. They left for your good. To make peace in the family, or so they told you. Some people get selfish as they grow up as a defense to being hurt. Anyway, we can and do go on with our own lives and let God judge them.

I didn't hate him. He was just someone I had known long ago. He was practically a stranger now. I had no real affection for him, but, as most kids from broken homes will tell you, there is a drive to know that absent parent. Maybe it is just to let them know you did ok without them. Of course, I never told my mom I was going to see him. I never wanted to hurt her.

After we went to see my dad, as fate would have it, he came to see us. I am sure he wanted to see my mom for whatever reason. Not sure he ever quit wanting her. He was very possessive and controlling when they were together. I told mom they were coming and she stayed upstairs in her bedroom so she would not have to see them.

She didn't like Gertrude because, when David was a teen ager and had gotten into trouble, my dad was ordered by the courts to pay delinquent back child support. Gertrude told the court that because she had a lot of medical bills they couldn't pay the child support. The judge sided with Mom and told Gertrude the kids were there before she was and they were my dad's responsibility.

We decided to take them out to dinner at the NCO club instead of visiting at the house so mom would be able to leave her room. Before we could leave, though, my dad managed to get upstairs to go to the bathroom. He opened the door to mom's room and said to her," Hell, Betty. You got old." She replied, "You don't look so hot yourself" and closed the door. She told me this later. He came back downstairs without our knowing this had happened. I decided then that Mom was the one important to me and my children and I would not see my father again if Mom were alive. That was the last time I saw him. When he was dying, I had moved to California. His step-daughter called for me to come. I told her he was a stranger to me. Mom and Gene needed me more at that time. I didn't go.

CHANUTE A.F.B. 1971-1975

Chanute was one of the top training bases for the Air Force. Gene loved his new job as an instructor. It made up his mind as to what he wanted to do when he retired. He wanted to finish school and teach automotive repair. He also liked the respect that went with being a Master Sergeant. He was now in the top three ranks of the NCO's. There were only two more stripes above his and he wanted to make them all. He worked very hard for the Air Force and for us. I was proud of all that he had accomplished. He deserved the respect he got.

Once again, he was chosen to play on the base softball team. We loved going to all his games and spending time with the other guys and their families. He was still playing first base when another guy ran into him, breaking his right arm. Gene's arm took an extra-long time to heal. The doctors were considering surgery when it started to heal and they finally took him out of the cast.That put him out for the season and ended his ball career as a player. He later became an umpire for the base teams and a coach for the boys' little league games. He liked umpiring and was very good at it. That is what he did from then on. He was thirty-nine then and the doctors told him it was time to quit playing and getting hurt.

Jim was a good catcher but, having been at all the ball games with his dad and listening to the older guys chide each other, he had picked up some bad habits like showing the ball to the batter after he caught it and gloating when the batter missed the ball. He soon learned this was not a good thing to do. A group of boys jumped him after a game and beat him up. He didn't tease them after that.

Jerry was more intimidated by Gene coaching his team. Gene would tell him what he was doing wrong and how to correct it. If Jerry would miss a ball coming to him, he would fall down and act as if he were hurt, so Gene wouldn't yell at him. Gene finally realized what was happening and took it easier on him. Jerry was that kid in right field. Some of you may remember that old song "Right field where the dandelions grow." The ball rarely gets hit to right field.

Gene and I had always liked to dance and the base had a square dance group. We had never square danced. We found it more fun than any other dancing we had done. We met a great group of people. There was also a group for teenagers and another for the younger kids. The whole family became square dancers. Jim and Beth both became callers and both were very good at it. There were other groups all over the Midwest and Illinois. Our groups would spend the weekends traveling to other towns to dance. We earned badges for dancing in odd places like jails and in the snow. There was no drinking at the dances.

We had to listen to the caller or we would mess up the whole set. If we messed up on one call, it was easy to mess up sober. Some did sneak out to their cars for refreshments, occasionally.

We loved dancing with this group from the base and sometimes there would be after parties at someone's house for the adults or we would all go out to eat after the dances.

We met our good friends, the Moutons, the Hemmerichs, and the Kreighs at these dances. These were life time friendships with them and their children. In fact, our son Jim married the Kreigh's daughter, Dianna.

We finally got base housing. We had a four bedroom with a basement. More room than we ever had. It was a duplex with adjoining carports. The fourth bedroom had a sliding divider that could make one big bedroom or two bedrooms. At first, we put the three girls in the one big bedroom and Mom had her own room. There was a room downstairs for the boys and tv room or den. Even room for company if we had any.

The family next door that we shared the carport with, the Hemmerichs, had six kids. I was a little nervous about how the kids would get along living that close. I was even more nervous when the father got home from work that first day. He was the biggest and loudest guy that I had ever lived so near to. When he spoke, his kids moved immediately and said, "yes, sir" and so did ours. I met his wife Sarah. She was a special lady. Right away Sarah said something like this, "Before you call the base police on my kids, would you talk to me first." I answered her with "I won't call the police on yours if you don't call them on mine." From that moment on, Sarah and I were sisters and soul mates, best of friends for life. Amazingly, we never had an incident between the kids that I can remember. They all remain friends to this day. Sarah was one of the hardest working people I had ever met. She was driving the base school bus when we met. Richard worked for Manpower in the Air Force. His job was to check on all the units to see that they used their personnel and money to the best interest of the Air Force. His position made him not well liked. No boss wanted someone else to tell them how to run their shop. Richard had the right personality for this job. He could care less if you liked him and he did his job well. He was an only child whose parents had immigrated from Germany. He wanted everything he did to make money. Of course, having six kids, he, like us, needed money. Sarah met Richard when she was just sixteen. He was eighteen; since he was older and wiser, he treated her as one of the kids. Richard was boss. She loved him even though he was loud and in charge. He must have had a tender side no one else was privileged to see but Sarah. She would often say how handsome and beautiful he was to her. She thought all of her children were beautiful too and perfect. All her children were very nice kids. Sarah loved everyone she met she never knew a stranger and everyone that knew her loved her.

All the teenage boys, at that time, wanted to let their hair grow long like the Beatles and other singing groups. No more military buzz cuts. I heard the commotion from the Hemmerich household but I needed to ask Sarah something.

I knocked on their door anyway. Sarah invited me in. Then, she asked me to look at Rick's hair. Rick, sixteen, was the oldest boy. Sarah asked me if I thought Rick's hair made him look like a "queer". Before I could answer, Richard bellowed out from the kitchen, "I don't give a damn what she thinks. He will cut his hair."

I said my goodbyes. My question could wait. I later told Sarah to never involve me in their arguments again. She didn't, but we did discuss them when we two were alone.

My boys wanted to let their hair grow too. I said shoulder length as far as I was willing to allow. Any farther and they should sleep with one eye open because I would visit them in the night with clippers. I guess I wasn't much different from Richard. I just used different methods.

The kids were all in school and I decided to go to work again. I wanted something that I could do from home and so did Sarah. We found a beauty school and enrolled. After a few months, I felt I was not going to be really good at this. I was paying them to teach me and I was working harder for them than I ever worked at a job and paying them to let me do it. I quit that school again and found a job at a locally owned telephone company in Champaign-Urbana. This town was about fifteen miles from the base. I drove it in the winter and found I really didn't need money enough to risk driving in the bad weather. One day in the Spring, I was on my way home when a tornado was coming. All the big trucks were stopping under the highway overpasses. I pulled in with them, scared to death. I made my decision right then to quit my job and stay home.

I think it was the very next day, Gene told me the base service station was hiring. That was the job I wanted, the same one I had in Tucson. I applied and was hired. No more driving off base. It was perfect. The boss was a short German-American guy, Stan Post, a great boss who became a good friend. All the men who worked there were the nicest guys to be around. If you walked up and heard something you shouldn't, they apologized. Hard not to utter profanity when you are working on cars. I found most men treated women the way the woman acted. If you were respectful, you got treated that way. Men don't talk petty about the others they work with. If they have something to say, they say it to your face. It is one of the qualities I most like in a man. They don't usually gossip, either.

One Friday night, the kids were all off doing something and Gene, Mom, and I were home alone. Gene was watching tv downstairs. Mom was up in her room and I was straightening up the kitchen. Gina came in and went upstairs. Suddenly, I heard Gene yelling for me to call the Air Police. I ran instead to the basement to see why.

Gene was holding a young man down on the floor. He was having a hard time keeping him there. Gina heard the commotion and came downstairs. She thought she recognized the guy as someone from the party she had just left. She was begging Gene not to call the police on him. She told us his parents had just been divorced and he was upset. Meantime Gene was is struggling to hold this guy down, who was is obviously out of his mind. The man on the floor was yelling something at Red, the dog, "Shut up, white man!" It dawns on me that, no matter who this guy was, he needs help and so did Gene. Gene was is saying "Damnit! call the AP's!" which I did. The AP's came and took the guy out strapped to a stretcher. As it turned out, he was not who Gina thought he was at all, but some young Airman from the base who had drunk something called "Everclear", 190% proof alcohol. He was totally out of his mind. The next day, the AP's brought the Airman to Gene at his shop and asked if he wanted him court martialed. The Airman apologized and said wanted to say he was sorry to our family. I didn't want him to come to the house again and Gene didn't press any charges. We never saw him again. We were just thankful no one was hurt.

Sarah and Richard and some of their kids started square dancing with us at the Rec Center. Not sure how much Richard enjoyed it, but he came. A short time later, they bought a house in the neighboring town of Rankin and moved away.

We still saw them but not every day like before. Sarah finished beauty school and opened a beauty shop in her house just like she planned. She did well and still drove the school bus too.

Vicky started spending time at the Pizza Hut right outside the base and had friends that worked there. We celebrated her sixteen birthday there and, shortly after that, she went to work at Pizza Hut. I liked having her working. At least I knew where she was most of the time and who she was with. I wasn't impressed with some of the friends she was making here. Our other kids would hang out there also.

When Gene was at Indian Mountain, Alaska he had met a guy named Al Papineau. Al and his family were assigned to Chanute AFB, also. The Papineau's had two boys, Skipper and Gary. They were the ages of Vicky and Gina. They started dating our girls.

Dianna Kreigh, Gina, and Jim had become friends from square dancing. Jim and Di started dating in high school.

Vicky, Skipper, and Dianna were all seniors at Rantoul High.

When it was time for the prom, they all wanted to go together. Instead of Skipper taking Vicky, he took Gina. Vicky took Gary and Di took Jim. Of course, once at the prom, they paired off the way they wanted.

(Top Left to Right) Jim Antoine, Gary and Skipper Papineau.
(Bottom Left to Right) Dianna (Kreigh) Antoine, Gina (Antoine) Polkinghorn, Vicky Antoine.

Vicky was the first high school graduate in three generations of our family. No one in my family or Gene's had graduated high school. This was a big occasion. Of course, we celebrated it at Pizza Hut.

The girls and the Papineau boys parted company after the Prom. They remained friends for life, as we did with their parents. Jim and Di continued to date after she graduated. Jim and Di always took Gina with them when they went out. No doubt they were fixing her up with someone or she was picking up her own dates from the Airmen she met at the Pizzeria on base. Not sure if Di and Gina just took Jim along for the car in the beginning, but eventually love won out and Jim and Di were married and are still together at this writing.

The Base opened a Pizzeria on base. Jim, Di and Gina all hung out there. I was comfortable with my kids hanging out at the Pizzeria on the base. Jim got his first job at sixteen, working on base at the Chow Hall. Gina got a job there too, right after her sixteenth birthday. Things were good.

Vicky met a young guy from Maine, Terry Swift, at the Pizza Hut. Terry had come to Chanute with his best friend who had enlisted in the Air Force. Not sure if Terry adopted our family or we adopted him. Terry became part of our family and would be connected to us for the rest of our lives.

There was one incident that could have altered that relationship while we were at Chanute. Gene and I had gone to see family in St. Louis on a weekend. One of the few times we didn't take our teenagers along. They had to work. We had just gotten Vicky her first car. It was a 1964 powder blue Buick, pristine condition.

On our way home, we saw Vicky's car sitting on the roadside in the next town, Thomasville. When we got home we confronted the kids as to why the car was there and why it was out of Rantoul. They were not to leave town while we were gone. Gina told us they had just driven to Thomasville and the engine overheated so they had to leave it there.

The next morning, we went to tow the car home. The more Gene and I thought about it, the more convinced we were that it could not have overheated in that distance.

Gina had gone off for the day to a gravel pit that the kids went swimming in called Kick-a-Poo with Terry and some friends. It was about forty minutes from home.

I questioned Vicky and Jim some more about the car. We found out Terry had been driving Vicky's car from that gravel pit at Kick-a-Poo Park when it overheated. This made more sense and, of course, I was angry that Gina had lied to us. I was going to Kick-a-Poo to kick some one's butt. Gene, of course, said wait for her to come home. There was no way I was going to let her enjoy this day. Gene wasn't coming with me so, I made Jim go with me to find her. When we got to Kick-a-Poo, Jim had me going in circles saying he couldn't remember exactly where the gravel pit was. I said, "Ok. Either you remember or you take the punishment." Five minutes later we parked the car at the gravel pit.

Below us, Gina and Terry were standing on the bank. I yelled, "Gina Renee, get yourself up this hill!" She came on a run and Terry dove into the gravel pit. Terry stayed away for a while until things cooled off. Gene set to work, repairing the engine with Jim's help.

Mom worried a lot about the kids and what they were doing. I eventually had to decide, that, for either of us to have some peace, I would have to move Mom to live by herself. She had Medicare now so doctors were no problem. She wanted to go to Missouri, closer to Beva and Sally and their families.

Before we could get this all arranged peacefully, there was one more big argument. Mom was so angry with me, she said that if I hadn't made her promise that she would not go back to Buck, my step-father, when I came to California, she might still be married and have a place of her own.

I packed Mom and her things in the car and she and I made the trip to St. Louis alone. She would not sit in the front seat beside me. I was driving the speed limit of seventy miles per hour on the highway. She began to fidget with the back door. This scared me as she had tried suicide once before. I truthfully did not know what she might do. I stopped to get gas and eat on the way but she would not even sit with me to eat.

Finally, we arrived in St Louis. Beva had a small travel trailer for mom to stay in. I stayed the night, said my goodbyes, and headed home.

After a month or so, Mom was complaining about the trailer. She couldn't stand the smell of the smoke in it. Someone had smoked in it and, with her emphysema getting worse, she was very sensitive to the smells. Beva thought she was just complaining for no reason.

Someone Beva and Robert knew had a small apartment for rent so they moved Mom in there. She seemed happy for a while but this apartment was right near a busy highway with lots of noise. Beva and Sally had to take her to the stores. Mom didn't want to ask them. She never liked having to depend on anyone. I came to St. Louis as often as I could and we went on as though nothing had happened between us.

I found another apartment shortly after that for her. It was somewhat nicer but was still close to the highway. People would tell Sally and Beva that they had seen Mom pushing a shopping cart along the highway. This would make both of them upset and cause them to worry. All she had to do was call and let them know she needed something. They were both close enough to take her to the store but she wouldn't ask. Being independent is the hardest part of getting old. I know I will not do it gracefully either and pray for my kids to understand.

It was the Spring of 1975 when Gene got orders to go to Korea. He had not been feeling well but the doctors couldn't find anything that would keep him from taking the assignment. They even put him in the hospital to check him out. I am convinced they thought his complaints were merely to get him out of his assignment. He complained of a heaviness in his chest and generally, not feeling well. He got his date to leave and we had to move out of base housing before he left. The family could not stay in base housing when the military person was gone. The military have changed this rule now. This was very hard on the family. Hard enough on the kids to have one parent missing and then to have to move out of their home too. The kids were great. They never complained. It had become their accustomed way of life to be always on the move. We found an old house in Rantoul to rent. A big, old white two-story building. This was the first house we had ever lived in. Up to now it had been apartments, base housing, or duplexes.

I wanted to keep working while Gene was gone. The kids had jobs and wanted to finish school there. The movers came and moved our belongings to the new house at 427 E. Sangamon, Rantoul, Illinois.

Vicky graduated high school and Gene left for Kunsan, Korea in May 1975.

* * *

CHAPTER THIRTEEN-KUNSANAFB KOREA - JUNE1975 –NOV 75

Gene left for Korea in June of 1975. Korea would change our lives forever. Both in good ways and bad.

Gene had his twenty years in for retirement and, looking back, we should have retired and never taken this assignment. He had set himself a goal to reach the highest rank he could. He only needed one more stripe to fulfill that dream. It was never to be. Still, he had achieved the highest rank of any Antoine in his family and that was quite an accomplishment.

Later, our son Jim could claim that honor, which only made Gene even more proud of Jim's career.

Gene's generation was the first to have ever served in the U.S. Military. His two older brothers served equally as well and retired after twenty years or more. His youngest brother did one tour in the U.S. Navy but decided the military life was not for him. The promotions were sometimes frozen so everyone, no matter how good they were, could not advance. All of them were honorably discharged and that alone is something to be very proud of.

Every letter I received from Korea from Gene, he complained that he did not feel well. He knew something was wrong. He was having medical problems that the Air Force doctors could not find or didn't look for. He felt no one was listening.

I had always relied on Gene to take care of us. My job was simply the kids and house. Today, I would not have just sat by and listened to his complaints. I would have insisted the doctors find the cause. I would have called a Senator, the Red Cross, the News Media, or anyone I thought would listen to me. I would have fought to get him home. He never asked and I was always hoping for the doctors to do their job.

To make matters worse, he was upset with this assignment because the job he was filling was for a T/Sgt. position. He was now a Senior Master Sergeant, S/SMSgt. This was two steps below the rank that he had worked so hard to achieve. The following are excerpts from Gene's letters to me from Korea:

August 24, 1975

"I went off base to a little town where the sisters of Good Shepherd have a school. I helped paint the school. School is out for the summer so a lot of the guys go out there on Sunday and paint. This is the first time I did it but plan on going again next Sunday. I walked two miles out there, two miles back, then ran a mile after I got back.

I think I would like to learn how to play tennis too. I if I had someone like you to play with. Really it would be good exercise. If I ever get this weight down again, I'm going to do everything I can to keep this weight down. That means exercise of some kind.

I really hate to see tomorrow get here because of all those blood tests I have to have taken. Hope I don't pass out. I told the doctor the last visit I had, that I want them to find out what is wrong with me. Why I get those infections, why I always feel tired, why I have pressure in my chest, and why my left leg keeps going numb.

I told him I didn't want to become a basket case before they found out what is wrong. This thing with my left leg just started since I have been here. I can be walking, which is when it happens most frequently, standing or sitting, and the thing goes numb.

I told the doctor this and I've mentioned it to some of the guys I work with. They all give you the feeling it is something I have made up just to get out of here. That's the biggest reason I hate to see a doctor. They always make me feel that my symptoms are different from any they have ever heard and never know what I have. Most people they can diagnose, but me, I'm a real odd ball. I know this pressure in my chest is there. I know I haven't always had it, so something is causing it. I know my leg goes numb and it didn't do that before. There must be something causing that too.

I think he feels my weight and stomach are causing my problems. He (the P A) said he will see what these blood tests show and if I am still having problems. He would send me to some Army base where they have a specialist and they can check me too.

I don't want you to worry about what I am telling you, or I won't tell you things like this anymore. I just needed to tell someone my problems that I know will believe what I say."

August 31, 1975

"The base isn't all that bad and my job is OK. It's just that the job I was sent here to fill is already filled. I know there are other bases in the states, Chanute is one of them, that don't have a Senior Master Sergeant in the vehicle maintenance shop. They have me filling a 7-level position that could be filled by a T/Sgt. When they downgraded that position from Master Sergeant, they should have canceled my assignment. If I had known this before I left, I would have written a letter to my Senator. I don't know if it would do any good now. I guess the Air Force can mark up another screwing they gave to one of their people. I am bitter about this. I feel this year was stolen from us. Well, honey, I have cried long enough on your shoulder, so will say, I love you.

I went to see the doctor again yesterday. The reason I'm telling you is because I know you will worry anyway. He thinks the numbness in my leg is caused by a diseased nerve. Now, he has to find out what is causing it. He gave me some vitamin B. He said vitamins are good *treatment for nerves. I was telling one of the guys I work with about it and he said he had similar symptoms when he was stationed in Japan. I asked him how they treated it and he said with vitamins. I have to admit this doctor acts concerned. I hope I don't regret saying that."*

September 6, 1975

"Do you realize we will be married twenty years next month? Do you also realize in two months, I'll be 42 years old? Never thought you would be married to an old man someday, did you? I'm beginning to feel it too. The doctor told me the other day that part of my problem is I am getting older. He really knows how to hurt a guy."

September 8, 1975

"I don't know if I told you the blood test I took didn't show I had anything. The doctor said the numbness in my leg was caused by a diseased nerve which could be caused by an advanced case of Syphilis or Diabetes, but the blood test ruled both of them out. I told him I was sure glad to know that! Anyway, the medicine he gave me seemed to be helping my leg. He said something is aggravating the nerve in my leg but, like the doctors there with the sores on my leg, he doesn't know what.? I'm going to live as though it's nothing to worry about."

September 18, 1975

"You don't have to worry about me seeing the doctor concerning my leg. I'm going to keep bugging him until it is corrected. The vitamins he gave me do help some, but they are not the complete answer. I'll have to give them a try. I have enough to last me about two more weeks. If I go back too soon, he would probably tell me I didn't give the vitamins time to work, right?"

November 26, 1975

"They are sending me to Clark AFB in the Philippines sometime soon. This doctor here wants me to see another doctor about my leg. I wanted you to know in case I write a letter from there. It would come

as a surprise. I sure hope it doesn't mess up our plans. This guy at the hospital said I would probably go there one day, see the doctor, and come back the following day. I think I'm going to try to talk the doctor out of sending me to Clark. , I'm afraid they will mess up our plans now that it is getting that close to the date we have been looking forward to. Anyway, I can always see a doctor while I'm in the states. Wish me luck in talking him out of sending me.

It seems like I have always got something to worry me. Just can't seem to put my mind at rest. I think I've been working too hard. I'm tired, I need to get away from here for a while. I need someone to love me and comfort me. You can do the job, I know. I need to see you and talk to you. I need to hold you and kiss you. I know once I get with you again my leg will be alright because you have that special cure for all my problems."

November 30, 1975

Today I received a Western Union mailgram from the Air Force:

"Colonel A.W. Gratch
Assistant for Casualty Matters
Air Force Military Personnel Center

Senior Master Sergeant Eugene J. Antoine has suffered a stroke and is hospitalized in Seoul, Korea. His condition is stable and he will be moved to the U.S. ASAP. You will be kept advised."

December 4, 1975

Today I received a second western union mailgram:

"Colonel A.W. Gratch
Assistant for Casualty Matters
Air Force Military Personnel Center

Reference my previous telegrams concerning Senior Master Sergeant Eugene J. Antoine. A report just received states that he is improving slowly and his condition is stable. His morale is good and he is alert but unable to speak. You will be kept informed."

(End of Gene's letters and letter from USAF)

During the time after Gene left for Korea, things at home were uneventful for the kids and me. Jim and Dianna started seeing each other again and were talking about getting married. Jim also signed up to go into the Navy after graduation.

On the weekend of Gene's stroke, the kids and I had driven to Missouri for Thanksgiving and my mom's birthday. We stayed at Sally and Don's.

I think the thirtieth of November was a Friday. The kids took the car to go visit with their other cousins. It was raining and I was uneasy about them being out on roads they weren't really familiar with.

Sally and I had sat up talking as we usually did when we were together. I remember her saying something about how blessed Gene and I were. We had not been spared all the anguish that goes with parenting, but our kids were fairly responsible and we had a good relationship. We had been blessed with a good life. Gene and I were looking forward to our planned meeting and second honeymoon in Hawaii. Tickets were bought and reservations made.

The next morning that world fell apart. My brother-in -law Robert came to Sally's with Gene's Mom. They brought the telegram from the Air Force to me. We were all devastated. I worried how Gene was, did he know what had happened to him? Would he ever recover from this? I knew if he were alert he would be waiting and wanting me to come to him as soon as I could. I wanted to go right then to where ever he was. The Air Force people couldn't tell me anymore than the telegram. They said I would miss him in flight if I tried to get to him in Korea. They would get him stable and air evacuate him to the states. The plane would be stopping at all the bases in between. I should just stay home until they finally got him to the states. I had never thought about not being able to get to him overnight. These were some of the hardest days I would ever have to live.

My two sisters Beva and Sally followed me and the kids home to Rantoul, to wait for the word when I could go. That took five days.

Finally, the Air Force told me on the fifth of December they would arrive at Travis AFB in California. I told them I would be there. I called my brother Bill in Jamul, California. Bill and Anna said they would drive to San Francisco and pick me up at the airport and get me to Travis.

Beva and Sally left to go back home to their families, leaving the kids alone. This was a big concern but I had to depend on them. They did know people to call if they needed anything. They had the Hemmerichs, the Moutons, the Papineaus, and my boss, Stan. I thank God for family and good friends. I do not know how one gets through life without God, family, and friends. I am so blessed and thankful for them all.

Bill, Anna and I got to the base before the air evacuation plane and were waiting at the hospital. When the ambulance bus arrived, I was allowed to go on it. When Gene saw me, all he could say was, "Oh, Boy! Oh, Boy!, Oh, Boy!"

We both cried and held each other. I knew mentally he was fine and, as bad as he looked, I felt he would recover. Maybe not be the way he was before, but that was not the important thing then. He was home, alive, and with me again.

At first, the hospital said I would not be allowed to go with Gene on the Med-evacuation plane. I threw a fit and told them after what we had been through this year, I was going to be on that plane with him, or as a patient myself. They got me a seat.

Bill and Anna left after they knew I could fly with him. I will always be indebted to them for being there for us. Thank You.

The next morning, we were loaded on the plane. Gene was on a gurney, but I could see him. I think we went to Texas, Michigan, and stopped overnight at Scott AFB, Illinois. While we were at Scott AFB, Gene's sister, Loretta, drove over from St. Louis and brought Gene's mom to see him. He was so happy to see them too. It made them feel better to know he was ok and he knew them.

Early the next morning, we were loaded up again and made the flight to Dayton, Ohio to Wright Patterson AFB. It is a regional Air Force hospital, so they were equipped to handle the stroke and his retirement orders if it came to that. We were sure it would be his last assignment.

Gene was admitted to the hospital at Wright Patterson and he was still unable to talk, read or write, but you could tell he understood all that was going on.

That first evening came and our next battle. Everyone told me I would not be allowed to stay in Gene's room at the hospital with him. I could not even imagine sitting alone in a hotel room, worrying about him and the kids in Illinois. I thought that would be more than I could handle. I knew he did not want me to go out of sight. I told them I was not leaving him. They got everyone from the Commander to the Chaplain to talk to me. They told me he needed his rest and I would be unable to help him if I didn't rest too. I refused to leave. They said they would have to put me on the third floor, which was for the mental patients. I refused to leave. Finally, they asked the man who was sharing the room if it would bother him if I stayed. He said, "Hell, No! You s.o.bs get out of here and leave her alone!" They finally did. I could have kissed him but thanked him instead.

We spent from the fifth of December until the twenty-fourth in that hospital. The kids drove over from Illinois a couple of times.

One time we were all singing Jingle Bells and Gene started to sing. He still couldn't talk but could say a little more than, "Oh, boy!" It wasn't always the right word but we tried hard to figure out what he was trying to tell us. He seemed to know sometimes when he used the wrong words. Cuss words were some of the first to return, reflex words. He might call a girl a boy or the dog a kitty and vice versa. It was always in the right category, though.

After a week or more, the doctors were talking about retiring him. They said he would be retired as incompetent because he would not be able to read the orders or sign his name. I would have to become his guardian. This was really upsetting to me. It was as if he would never get better. I knew he was not incompetent. He knew very well what was happening. I had watched him watch football on tv. He knew everything that was going on. When it comes to football, I am still the incompetent one.

They just didn't want to keep him in the hospital and give him the therapy he would need. By this time, he was gaining strength and could get from the bed to a lounge chair. He still could not walk and needed a wheelchair. The fact that he was only forty-two and strong before all of this happened was in our favor.

Also, because his played sports, using his left hand to hit a baseball and golf ball, helped too. I encourage everyone to make a habit of using your less dominant hand to do things. You never know when you may need it.

I called my friend Sarah and told her what was going on. She called her husband, Richard, who was going to law school in Chicago at that time. Richard had retired from the Air Force. He drove all night to come to Wright-Patterson to help me talk to the doctors and slow down this process. Finally, the doctors had a conference with me and said if I could get Gene to be able to sign his name, they would give us a little more time.

Richard and I thought I should go home and get the bank accounts set up in my name and make sure I wouldn't have to account to the Air Force for every quarter I gave the kids. We left that night for Rantoul. I realized for the first time that Richard was a very caring man and whata good friend he was to me. I don't think up to that time we had ever had a conversation. It was always Sarah and I doing the talking.

I went to see the doctors at Chanute AFB hospital and they said they would take Gene as an outpatient. They would give him speech therapy so we could slow down the retirement process. I took our van back to Wright-Patterson with the intention of bringing him home for Christmas and keeping him there. Wright Patterson agreed with the plan except that I was to admit Gene to Scott AFB after Christmas.

We got to Rantoul and had an ordeal getting Gene into this house. There were a few steps up to the front door. The kids were all there and their friends to help. Gene's mom had come over from Missouri to spend Christmas with us and Sally was there too. I remember very little about those first day's home, except I knew Gene was going to stay home with us from then on. We found we could manage. His mother wanted to stay and take care of him too. I guess I was not thinking about her feelings at the time. He was her baby. My thoughts were that she would keep him depending on her and not make him try to help himself. I told her I would look for an apartment close enough for her to come every day if she wanted, but I didn't want her to live with us right then. It hurt her feelings, which was not my intention.

I had just moved my mom to live by herself because it was so hard to deal with everyone's emotions. With five teenagers, a sick husband, and I not functioning well myself.

We had a good Christmas and the next morning, Gene's mom (Lula or Lou as we called her) asked me to take her to the Greyhound Bus station. She was going home to Missouri. I told her I was sorry, but she insisted on going home.

In the months that followed, Gene gained strength and became able to walk. He drew pictures and tried to write some words. The speech therapy was helping some, but we had a long way to go. He didn't always spell words right but sometimes thought he did. He sometimes was sure he said the right words but didn't and would get upset with us if we couldn't figure out what he was trying so hard to tell us. This was by far the biggest challenge for all of us.

One day, listening to the radio, I heard Mel Tellis, the country singer, telling a story about being robbed. For those who never heard of Mel Tellis he was a very good singer, but he stuttered badly when he talked, yet, he never stuttered when he sang. He said he had to sing for help because of his stuttering.

I wondered if Gene would be able to say his name if we sang it. So, on the way to therapy and, every time we could, we would sing,

"My name is Eugene James Antoine,
427 East Sangamon, Rantoul, Illinois. "

It didn't take too long before he could say that without singing it! We practiced every day writing his name until he could do it when asked. The Air Force put him on a temporary retirement which was to last five years to see if he would recover and be able to work. This meant we had to go every year to be tested to see what he could do and if he could be employed. Social S Security Disability had was the same requirements.

This was not bad but we worried about what kind of job they would make him take and what our income might be when they finally retired him, a sort of Limbo not knowing what to expect. I continued to work as Gene got better and was able to walk around the house without help. The kids were in and out through the day, so he wasn't alone too much. My boss was good to let me off for all the doctor visits. My job was only five minutes away from the house and Gene could dial the phone. He couldn't say much more than hello, but I would know if he needed me.

As he progressed, I decided to see if he could still drive. I know if he had been fifty or older, I would never have even considered this. Being young and daring, we did. We went to a school parking lot and practiced. Amazingly, he was driving after only a few months of the stroke. I never reported the fact he'd had the stroke to the Insurance Company or the DMV. We just picked up where we left off. Thank God, he never had an accident or we would have been in some serious trouble. We didn't let him drive alone very often. Not because he couldn't, but, if he got stopped, he couldn't explain what happened and would surely be blamed for the accident or accused of drinking.

One accident occurred that was not his fault at all. I had driven Vicky's Buick to work to get the oil changed. I noticed the brakes felt mushy and funny and had asked the guys to check them. They didn't get to it because they were busy that day. The next day I totally forgot about it. I told Gene to drive it to the station and go to lunch with me.

My office at the service station had been a storeroom with no windows or back door. I heard what sounded to me like an explosion out front of the station. My first thought was gas exploding. I ran from the office, thinking of how many times I had asked Stan to at least put in a window so I could get out if there was an emergency. I saw Gene, walking and upset through the garage. He was shaking his head and wringing his hands. The brake master cylinder had gone out on the Buick just as he was parking the car at the end of the garage. The car plunged forward, took out a portion of the wall, and almost hit one of our mechanics. Thank God, only the building, which was aluminum, was damaged. The Buick was like a tank, not a scratch on it.

The Air Force Police came to investigate. I did some fast talking, answering all their questions. I could see the police were very annoyed with me doing all the talking. They wanted the "Sarge" to talk not me. Finally, we got our Insurance Company to pay the damages and all ended well.

Then there was that first ticket for speeding. Gene had gone to watch Matthew Hemmerich, one of Sarah's boys, play ball. Matt said he was so scared because he knew Gene couldn't talk. The cop came to the window and said, "You were speeding." Gene just gave him his driver's license, took the ticket, and didn't say anything at all. Matt was very relieved but he didn't want to drive with Gene after that ordeal.

When it was time for Gene to renew his license, we did tell them he couldn't read the test. They said that was ok. He took the be-hind- the- wheel test and they asked him oral questions which, thank God, he answered right.

There were many other tests for his driver's license but he al-ways passed. He was an excellent driver until he died. Never had to give it up. I was so thankful for that and the fact I had let him try. It was the one thing in life he truly enjoyed doing. He had such a fabulous memory, always knew which lane to be in. He drove many times across the U.S. He drove in the heavy traffic of New York City and Los Angeles. Never had any trouble but did get a couple more speeding tickets.

After he passed his first renewal test, we did tell the insurance company about his stroke. It was never an issue.

We started playing Bingo to help with numbers. At first this was hard. I had to watch his cards and mine. He had to actu-ally see the numbers because he could not understand the call-ers. If they said "five" he would cover six. The brain works so fast. When he would count, he always went one number further than he meant to. When the Bingo didn't have the tv monitor to show the numbers, I would have to write them on a paper for him. He adapted very quickly to this. Even though I am not crazy about bingo, it was an entertainment he could enjoy. All his memory, short and long, was now fine. He knew car engines and knew what needed to be done to repair them. Everything he had ever learned was there. His long-term memory was great. I thanked God many times that we had met and married young. His memories were mine too and all his friends were my friends so he could give me one word and I could tell his stories for him. I must admit, sometimes I would get tired of this role or would think what he had to say wasn't that important. I am so sorry for that. I realize now that everything was important for him to communicate to us and the world.

He always worked so hard to make all our lives easier. Dancing was not always easy for him, but he would dance, at first for me, then because people complimented us. He enjoyed it too. He was a very good dancer in his day. He loved music. It didn't matter if it was the old songs we both loved or something modern the kids listened to. He knew all the artists, even the new ones after the stroke like Barry Manilow, Santana, and Neil Diamond. I never knew any after 1956 when I had my first baby. I hardly learned the lyrics to any song after that. He couldn't always sing the lyrics until someone would give him the first word, but he had it after that.

He loved to sing. We sang everywhere we went in the car. He would start to hum the melodies, then wait for me to get the words. It became a game of guessing what song is this. Music went through his head day and night, I think.

The hardest thing for Gene to give up after the stroke was going to work and having a job. For at least five years or more, when we were on an Air Force base, we would have to go see the vehicle maintenance shops. He had to see if there were any of the guys he had worked with still around and to just talk to the guys that ran things. After most of the guys he had worked with retired, he finally quit going to the shops.

As our communication skills got better, Gene told me about what had happened in Korea. He and a Korean he worked with on the base had gone to a club for dinner. He thought he may have had a drink but didn't remember drinking anything. The next thing he remembered was the Korean man helping him into a cab and telling the driver where to take him. He went straight to his room.

The next morning, he still didn't feel well but thought if he ate breakfast he would feel better. Some other Sergeant spoke to him and he realized he couldn't answer him. He walked to the NCO club and collapsed outside the door. Someone called for help and took him to the ER. From there they took him by ambulance to another base in Seoul, Korea, two hours away. That is when they decided he had had a massive stroke. So, he had two strokes.

I often wonder how that Physician Assistant felt when he finally knew there had been something happening all the time.

There was a note in Gene's medical file from the Physician Assistant that stated he could not sort out Gene's complaints and that Gene seemed upset that he was not with his wife. We think that was the only thing they were concerned about was Gene simply wanted to go home.

* * *

CHAPTER FOURTEEN-LEAVING RANTOUL, ILL 1976

In May of 1976, our oldest son, Jim, graduated high school and joined the Navy. He and Dianna wanted to get married before he left for his Navy training.

Dianna's family were retired now from the Air Force and lived in West Plains, Missouri.

Both of our families were from Missouri. We asked the priest at the church, St. Joseph's in Kimmswick, Missouri if we could have the wedding there. It was at the same church where Gene and I had gotten married in twenty years before. The priest agreed to perform their wedding.

My sisters, Beva and Sally organized everything. They rented the hall for the reception and prepared all the food. We had purchased a travel trailer so we loaded all the wedding supplies in the trailer and caravanned to Missouri. Gene, the girls, and I stayed at Sally and Don's. We found a camp ground close by for the boys and the trailer. My good friend, Sarah Hemmerich was still working as a beautician. She came with us and fixed all the girls' hair for them.

The wedding had a few glitches. Rich Avis, the father of the flower girl and one of Gene's nephews came in just after the priest got to the altar. Rich was hurrying down the aisle with the little girl in his arms. The flower girl was five minutes late and the priest would not wait for them. Of course, they were disappointed.

They had probably spent money they couldn't afford to pay for the dress she wore. Richie apologized and we assured him it was ok. Things happen at all weddings, no matter how well they are planned.

It was a beautiful wedding with all those we loved there.

That evening everyone that wanted to went on the river boat, the Admiral. The Admiral was a huge paddle wheel boat that took tours up and down the Mississippi River for years. It had a full orchestra and ballroom for dancing.One of the all-time great things to do in St. Louis. It is now a gambling casino and stays docked on the Mississippi River in St. Louis.

Lula Wefer, Gene and Jo Ann Antoine, Betty Bainter

The next day, the wedding party and all their friends spent the day at Six Flags over the Mid-America, an amusement park.

We returned to Rantoul and Jim left for his Navy training in San Diego. The same Navy Training Center Gene had gone to twenty years earlier. Dianna stayed with us. We were already planning a trip to San Diego in September for Jim's graduation from boot camp.

Sometime in late August or early September of 1976, we received a call from Sally. Our brother David, in a drunken rage, had shot and killed two people. This came as a complete shock to all of us, especially Mom. David had not been in any real trouble since he was a teenager. He was thirty-five in 1976. He had started his own business and it was doing very well. We were all so proud of him. Mom had written a poem for him called, "My Son, the Business Man."

My Son, the Businessman
By Betty Bainter

Are you talking to me about that chap?
The one who has the infectious laugh.
The one with personality-plus,
On the other side of the room from us.

The one who is short, handsome, and cute.
Wearing a pretty light brown suit.
He has a business here in town, you say.
A hard worker, and he's doing OK.

Well, I'm not surprised; I predicted it so.
In a poem, I'd written back long ago.
He's come a long way from yesterday,
And the hard knocks, he got along the way.

From life's stormy sea where he tumbled and tossed,
From the bridges, he burned and the roads he crossed,
To surmount all those obstacles placed in his way,
It took courage to get where he is today.

So, if you're asking me if I know that chap,
The one who has that infectious laugh.
The one clean shaven, neat as a pin,
Well, yes, I believe I do know him.

Though not as well as I one time did,
When he was a snotty-nosed, dirty-faced, ragged jean kid.
I will pray for him you until I can no longer pray,
That he will let God be his your master, day after day.

Mom's heart was broken that day and she would never get over the pain.

This is David's account of what happened.

Earlier that day, David had offered the young man he shot a job. The guy said he didn't like David and didn't want to work for him. Later, after drinking, David stopped at a woman's house next door to this same guy. The woman told David to leave because he was drunk. She went next door and got her neighbor to tell David to leave. This angered David because of the earlier conversations.The guy told David if he didn't leave, he had a gun and David would leave one way or the other. David then left and went to his trailer and got a gun someone had given to him. He returned to the woman's house with the gun. By this time, the woman had the owner of the trailer park, Charlie to come to her trailer. Charlie was sitting at the table when David came in and said," Who is going to shoot who?" The guy David had argued with lunged for the gun in David's hand. It went off and shot Charlie in the eye. David thought Charlie was dead. David panicked and shot the other guy. That guy's girlfriend started yelling hysterically and running away. David turned the gun on her and fired.
Realizing what he had done, David left the park and called Sally from a phone booth. He told Sally he was in terrible trouble and he needed money to run away. Sally knew he was in big trouble of some kind. She and Don took what money they had to him. When they saw him, they realized he was distraught and was in real trouble but didn't believe he had actually shot someone. They gave him the money and left. They drove home and, by the time they got home, David called again. He was not going to run and wanted them to come get their money before he went to the police so they would not be involved. It was too late. Sally could hear the police arriving at the phone booth.

Robert, Beva's husband was a Deputy Sheriff in that county. He took the phone and talked to David. When he arrested David, he took Sally's money from him. Robert gave the money back to Sally to keep her and Don and their five kids from being involved. He convinced David it would go easier on him to plead guilty. David did.

We sold off David's business supplies and made a thousand dollars for a lawyer. The lawyer, of course, took David's money and wanted us all to get more. None of us had any more money to spare and had families of our own to care for. This lawyer never defended David any more than a public defender would have.

David was sentenced to two life sentences in prison. Charlie lost the sight in his eye but lived.

At this same time, Mom was in the hospital in St. Louis with emphysema. Since we were going to California for Jim's graduation, we thought we could take her with us, and she would never have to know what had happened.

My brother Bill lived in California and she could stay with them for a while. We called the hospital and asked them to keep her away from the tv and the news. The only place without a tv in that hospital was the mental ward. When they tried to move Mom there, she refused to go. She got so upset, the doctor took it upon himself to tell her what had happened. We took her from the hospital to Sally's. She agreed there was nothing we could do for David and she would go with us to California.

Once more, we were going cross-country. By the time we got to El Paso, Texas, Mom was getting sick again. We tried to get her on an airplane to Bill and Anna's, which would have only taken only a couple of hours. There were no flights for seven hours from El Paso and it was only seven hours farther on to Tucson, Arizona. We didn't want to put her in the hospital in Texas. We had no one to stay with there.

We had her lie down on the bed in the trailer so she could

be more comfortable. We drove on to Tucson and got her on a flight to San Diego. We went to a camp ground because she wanted to take a bath. I had never used the shower in a trailer and didn't realize there was only a small amount of hot water. Of course, the water turned cold before we finished the shower. It was terrible for her because she was already sick. I heated water on the stove as quickly as I could to finish bathing her. We finally got her to the airport. Bill picked her up in San Diego and took her straight to the hospital. She was still in the hospital when we arrived and stayed there several more days.

We made Jim's graduation ceremony. He was so handsome in his uniform, as all sailors are. He had orders immediately to go to Memphis, Tennessee. He and Di had a few days with us, then they were on their way to their new home and life.

Mom recovered from this ordeal and came home to Bill's. They had a very small house, but we had plenty of room in the trailer since Jim and Di were gone.

After a short time there, Bill suggested we try to buy a house or some property near them. That way we could both look after Mom. He could help me too. We had no plans now since Gene was going to be retired permanently at some point. I had tried unsuccessfully to buy a house in Rantoul. We really did not want to retire there. Vicky and I both liked our jobs but the more we thought about it, the better it sounded to us to stay in the San Diego area and near Bill.

We still had to return to Rantoul to have the military pack our belongings and put them in storage. I had told my boss, Stan that I was not sure I would be back. I didn't want to leave him in a lurch because he had been so good to me after Gene's stroke. I was going to give him my two weeks notice. Vicky could transfer with Pizza Hut and didn't want to be by herself in Rantoul. She quit her job also. Gene, Vicky, and I left to go take care of the move. The other kids stayed behind at Bill and Anna's. None of the kids objected to the move. It seemed we were all happy about it.

My brother Bill had a real estate friend, Bernie Wissel. Bill had done lots of work for Bernie. Bill called Bernie and he began looking for property in the area where Bill lived. We were about to give up finding anything when Bernie called to tell us that the Winnetka ranch, just up the road from Bill's, had four lots for sale. We looked at it and decided to buy one of the eight-acre parcels.

Bill had always worked in construction. He was a heavy equipment operator. He had cleared land and would help us build a house. He would frame the house for us. Gene, the kids, and I would do whatever we could to help build the house. Bill was convinced we could do this with his help. We would have to build it one step at a time because we had nothing to offer as collateral to get a loan. We had very little cash left after buying the land. We did own our car but not the trailer we were living in. What were we thinking? We had never bought anything valuable except a car and the travel trailer.

It was settled. We were going to do this. We picked the lot we wanted and started the process of buying. After deciding on the parcel, Bernie came to us, upset. His company had made a deal with another couple and it fell through. They wanted the same parcel we had chosen. Bernie showed us another parcel and we took it. Although we were upset, this was going to be in our favor years from that time.

* * *

CHAPTER FIFTEEN-TRIP
BACK TO RANTOUL-1977

FINISHING THE HOUSE

Gene, Vicky, age twenty, and I were on our way back to Rantoul, Illinois November 1976. We had to build a house on the property we had bought in California. We needed to put our household goods in storage and quit our jobs.

We stopped to get gas and have breakfast somewhere in Texas. After breakfast, Vicky said she needed to tell us something. I could tell it was serious and thought to myself "Oh, No! She is pregnant." It happens in most families and we had not yet had to face that. I was so relieved when she said, "Penny totaled my car." It was only a car.

We had allowed a young girl, Penny, who needed a place to live, to move into our home. Penny had just gotten a new job when we left on our trip to California and couldn't go with us. We told Penny she could stay at the house and use Vicky's car while we were gone. She was only to drive the car to work and home. She was also to take care of our dog the German shepherd named Red. Penny was not hurt in the accident and the car was replaceable. When we got to the house, we found Red in the garage. It was a mess. Red evidently had not been let out to go to the bathroom for days, probably not fed or watered either.

Penny had some other girl in the Air Force staying at the house with her. She and this girl had celebrated Penny's birthday and were drinking when Penny wrecked the car. Thank God neither was hurt, but that beautiful 1964 Buick was totaled.

I was so angry at Penny I could not even talk to her. I told her to get all her things out of our house and not come back. She did and we never saw her again.

Our friends, the Moutons had just retired and moved to a farm in Kentucky. While we were getting things done in Rantoul, they offered to take Red to the farm with them. We were going to stop there and pick him up when we started back to California.

John called us about a week later and told us Red had died. John felt really bad. He thought Red had eaten a frog and been poisoned by it. I think Red got sick when Penny didn't take care of him. Still, the dog's dying had upset John.

I told John, God is good because we were going to have to stay with my brother Bill until our house was built. Bill didn't have any dogs and didn't want any so this was probably a blessing in disguise.

It was enough to ask of Bill and Anna to have all of us and Mom there. He and Anna had no children either and we left three of our kids with them while we were in the process of moving and building. Bill had a very small house so the kids stayed in our travel trailer. They were all teenagers, but Bill was pretty stern so they behaved.

We got back to California just in time for Christmas. I mentioned that Bill and Anna had a very small house. In fact, the house had originally been a shed or even a chicken house and had only one bedroom. They were using a truck camper for their kitchen. Bill had put in a bathroom and later added a kitchen.

It was a work still in progress.

Bill had also built a huge work shop for his heavy equipment. He and Anna had their bed out in the shop. Bill had put the bed on wheels so he could move it out of his way if he was working there. He teased Anna, that it would be convenient on wheels in case he let her work in Tijuana as a call girl.

"Have bed, will travel," he said.

Mom was sleeping in the little house and we lived in our travel trailer. It was not uncomfortable and the winter was mild in California.

Bill and Anna went all out that Christmas for the kids. Bill got the biggest tree he could find and put it out in the shop. Anna and the kids had made the decorations and baked Christmas cookies. It was great.

Anna's mom, Irene and stepfather, Roger Temple lived on the same property. They had the main house. They were the cutest couple. Irene was just too cute and always had a smile. Roger was a mixture of Mr. Magoo and the Kentucky Fried Colonel. Roger and Irene married after Anna's dad died in 1966.

Bill and Roger had built a bar in Roger's barn. They christened the bar "The Hollow Leg". They hung a mechanical mannequin's hollow wooden leg over the bar with a net stocking on it. We would spend many New Year's eves at the "Hollow Leg" together in the years to come.

Anna's brother, Billy, his wife and family lived on property next to Bill and Anna's. They had four kids. Their kids and ours became friends and thought they were cousins because Anna and Bill were Aunt and Uncle to both families. My brother Bill became "Uncle Bill" and Anna's brother Bill became "Brother Bill" to end the confusion. Roger and Irene became Grandpa and Grandma Temple to all the kids on both sides.

This mountain was starting to feel like "Walton's Mountain", which was a new TV show at the time.

Roger had his property near the old Winnetka ranch long before he and Irene had married. When his first wife became sick, he worked on the ranch to be closer to home. After his wife died, he went to work at the San Diego Zoo. Roger was caretaker for "Albert", one of the San Diego Zoo's most famous gorillas.

Albert was still alive when we came to San Diego.

Roger and Irene were introduced to each other by a mutual friend who knew Roger and Irene's husband.

Roger met and worked with a retired Navy guy named Chick Schweers. Chick and his wife Mim later bought land and built on Mother Grundy Truck Trail too when Chick retired from the zoo. Roger and Chick's boss at the Zoo was another retired Navy guy named Bill Cryster. Bill Cryster and his wife Ricky also moved up on Mother Grundy Truck Trail. They built their house between Uncle Bill and Brother Bill's place.

Down the road a piece lived Bill and Joyce Weller, who would later became part of our family and friends. Our son Jerry married Annette Weller.

There were seven guys named Bill living on our dirt road, Mother Grundy Truck Trail. I dubbed all these guys "The Hill-Billy's". These were our new neighbors and friends and family. We were so lucky to spend many years with them.

We had the best New Year's Eve parties ever at the Hollow Leg. We even got to name our dirt road after Roger Temple. Temple Trail.

Aunt Anna found this little article from Winnetka, Illinois. The most famous "Winnetka" is now an affluent suburb of Chicago's North Shore.

It seems to describe our section of the Winnetka Ranch when we came to it. There was a story told at dinner parties in Winnetka about a little boy who was asked by his teacher to write about the Great Depression. Here's the write-up. It made me laugh.

"Once upon a time there was a Great Depression.

Everybody was poor.

The Father was poor.

The Mother was poor.

The children were poor.

*The cook was poor. The maid, chauffeur, gardener,
and nurse were all poor.*

It was very sad.

*It was sad but the servants stayed because unemployment
was so high*

there were no other opportunities available.

There was not a lot of money to go around. "

❋ ❋ ❋

CHAPTER SIXTEEN- THE WINNETKA RANCH AND BUILDING OUR HOUSE

The Winnetka Ranch had been a working ranch for years. No one had ever lived or built on it, but now it was divided into parcels that were being sold.

We closed escrow on the eight acres.

Remember, Gene was recovering from his stroke and couldn't help me make decisions.

I had never made these kinds of decisions in my life. Our biggest purchase up to now had been a car and travel trailer.

I thank God I was young then because today I would not have tried to do all that we did.

Mom was sick and we needed to get her settled. David had overwhelmed us all with what he had done.

On top of all that, we had no place of our own to live and we still had three teenagers at Home.

JUNE 1977 — DRILLED THE WELL

My brother, Bill and Anna's brother, Billy Reed had drilled wells before for a man named Bob Harris who owed them a favor. They borrowed his well drilling rig to drill our well. This was an exciting and scary time. It was like drilling for oil and spending your last penny on that venture; like putting your last dollar on that big spinning wheel at a casino. If we didn't get water, we could not build on the property we had bought. We had very little money left after buying the property. We had to save wherever we could. We had to pay the expenses for the well but Bill and Billy would supply the labor for nothing. Bill helped a lot to take the pressure off me. He got all the permits and dealt with the County inspectors.

We took lawn chairs and sat and watched the drilling every day. We prayed as we sat there. It was truly an emotional time. As I recall, they were still drilling when the moon began to shine the night we hit water. It was magical. When they hit the water, we were as excited as if it were gold. We had about thirty-five gallons a minute, more than enough to build on. One more prayer answered. God does work in mysterious ways. Only He could have known how many people would depend on that well in the years to come. It is a little hard to remember all the details of this now.

The next thing we had to do after the well was in was to get the electricity to the property. No one had ever lived on this part of the ranch so there was no electricity to it.

Bill had also bought a bulldozer and now he had to go to work to pay for it. So he could not do all we needed done. Building was going to be delayed.

After drilling the well for us, Bill told me we had to set up a temporary pole for the electric meter before the electric company would bring in the transformer for the electricity. This pole had to be sunk five feet into the ground. Bill could not help us do this. He gave me tools and a digging bar that weighed at least ten pounds.

Gene and I started to dig this hole. Gene had been right handed before the stroke. His right side was still partially paralyzed. It came back a little but he had to use his left hand as his dominant hand. He sometimes would forgot to move his right hand out of the way and just let it hang. This was dangerous at times. I would have to watch him closely and tell him to move his right hand; for instance, when it was close to the fan on the car he was working on. He just didn't pay attention to that side of his body. He dragged his right foot when he walked so had to be careful about falling. He still had a lot of weakness when we moved here. He had no strength and could not lift the digging bar with one hand. That meant I was going to do this. Gene did what he could with his one good hand. I, who had never done a real hard day's work in my life began to dig this hole. The digging bar weighed at least ten pounds. At first, it felt like a ton. We started to dig, inch by inch, shovel by shovel. I worried I was asking too much of Gene. He was still gaining strength and I didn't want him to have another stroke. It was very slow and I am not sure how long it took.

Bill had gotten us an electric pole, not sure how or from where. The pole had to be five feet into the ground. My height is five feet, two inches. The ground on this hill is decomposed granite. Until it is wet, it is solid rock. The well was not yet working to pump water from, so the water had to be carried in a bucket.

Someone told us that the electric company might dig the hole for us, so I called and they said," No."

The person that told me that had just gotten lucky that the guys from the electric company were in the area working and had done it for him. We could have rented an auger but Gene couldn't use it with one hand and I was afraid to try that. We could have hired someone to dig it for us but money was an issue.

We had to be careful with what we spent or we couldn't even build the house.

I started the hole about three feet across but, by the time I got almost to the bottom, it got narrower and narrower. When I had dug it out as much as I could, it measured only four feet, six inches deep. The hole was too narrow for me to bend over and dig any more dirt out of it. I knew Bill was making me do it all this to County Code and the County Inspector had to approve it.

Finally I was cleaning out the bottom of the hole with a coffee can and my head between my knees. I decided this was as deep as this hole was going to get. I had mud everywhere, even in my hair. An old song kept going through my mind, "If my friends could see me now". I got out of the hole and told Gene to get the tape measure. He did. The hole was four feet, six inches. Gene said, "Not good enough. Bill?" I said, "We are not going to tell Bill. We are going to roll the pole close to the hole. Then, we are going to back our station wagon close to the end of the pole. Then, you and I are going to put one end of the pole on the back of the roof rack of the station wagon and the other end near the hole. Then you are going to back up very slow until the pole falls into that hole. Then we will pile dirt up around it so if they measure the pole from the top it will be buried five feet."

Gene looked at me as if I had lost my mind but agreed to try it. I told Gene a couple of times that if I died, just shovel the dirt over me and leave me there. I knew Bill would not approve but I could not dig another six inches in that hard ground.

Hallelujah! It worked! The pole slid into the hole. No damage to the car, none to Gene and me. It was very heavy lifting the pole onto to the car, but I had developed many muscles digging that hole. Bill told us we had to put a metal pipe in the hole for a ground wire. We did that and filled it in as planned. That evening, we told Bill it was finished. Bill went up to check it all out. When he came back, he said, "that hole is only four feet-six inches deep." I asked him how he could tell that. He said the same way the electric company will. They will put a tape measure down that ground pipe. I was upset but we agreed to take our chances with the inspector. There was no way I could dig that hole deeper or again.

This was not the end of the digging and work for Gene and I to do. There were all the water lines and electric lines to be laid from the well to the house. Bill rented a trencher which he ran to dig the ditches. Gene and I had to clean out the excess dirt that fell back into the trenches. The trenches were thirty-six inches deep. For me that meant laying down on my stomach to be able to reach the bottom of the trench, to scrape out what fell back into it after the shovel had removed what it could. The pipes had to lie level so they would not crack or break when the weight of the water was in them. Gene used the shovel especially made for trenching. The well was 250 feet from the house. That was a lot of trench to clean and pipe to lay. Gene and I carried the pipes to the trenches and Bill did all the gluing them together. You had to do the gluing very quickly so the glue didn't set up or harden too soon. I guess we did a great job. It's been over forty years and only one pipe broke because a tree root wrapped around it.

Things were not looking good at this point. It would take us years to finish a house with Bill working. All this was beginning to seem so foolish and I was tired. Building our house was getting delayed. Finally, I decided it was never going to happen.

In April of 1978, I was talking to a neighbor, Ken Davis who had just built a new house down the road. I told him I was going to try to sell the property and move into town. Ken told me about a company called Palm Homes in Chula Vista that built houses.They were cheap houses, nothing fancy and had only a few floor plans to choose from. He gave me the phone number and I called them. They set up an appointment. The cheapest house they built was two bedrooms, one Bath and a one car garage. It cost $17,500 completed. Dry walled and everything. They already had the plans approved by the County and it would only take a couple of months to complete.

It was too good to be true. We talked finances next. They needed the whole $17,500 before they would start. We only had $10,500 left and nowhere could we borrow the rest. They said come back when you have all the money. Gene and I were both so elated at first but so depressed when we left there.

I went back to Ken with what I was told. He asked me if we had any insurance policies we could borrow on. We had two very old Prudential and Metropolitan family policies. We had been paying six dollars and fifty cents or so a month on them for many years. Ken said call them and see what they will loan. I did. On one, we could get $1200 and on the other $1300. Now we had $12,500.

I went back to Palm Homes. They said no, all or nothing. We came home to Bill's, not knowing what to do next. That evening the phone rang. It was the salesman from Palm Homes. He said they had decided to carry the last $5000. They would start work immediately. I can't tell you the feelings we experienced then. There are no words except, "Thank God."

When they came out to the site for the house to lay out the plans, the electric pole was in the way for their plans, and would have to be moved. Life is hard. We dug a second hole and this one was the full five feet deep.

The electric company set their one main pole for the transformer and hooked up the electricity to the well and work began on the house.

Palm Homes

We went every day to watch the progress of the house building. It was all so exciting. One day, I noticed a circle drawn above the outside door in the garage. Someone had written the word "Think" in the circle. It remained a mystery until the house was finished. Then, we realized the door from the house and the door in the garage could not be opened at the same time. Mystery solved. It really was not a problem, as we later remodeled and took the garage door out anyway.

The house was finished and ready to move into in May of 1978.

We were finally home.

At last, two vagabonds had a permanent residence for the first time in both our lives. With the house finished, we made arrangements to have our household goods delivered from storage. Seeing all our familiar furniture and belongings was like Christmas. It made the house ours.

"Ant Hill" Est. 1978. Jamul, CA

Gene, Gina, Jerry, Beth, and I moved into the house. The two girls had the second bedroom and we fixed Jerry a room in the garage. We had never intended to use the garage as a garage but as extra living space until when we could remodel it.

Mom was improving some and wanted to move to live by herself. We found a cute little apartment for her and she moved to El Cajon.

Vicky got a job at Pizza Hut and moved in with Mom so she could get too work. She didn't have a car yet. Without God's guidance, none of this could have happened the way it did. God brought us to this mountain and knew exactly what our future held.

1978 — ANT HILL, CALIFORNIA

Jim finished his Navy school in Memphis. He and Dianna came back to San Diego. He was stationed at Miramar Naval Air Base.

They found an apartment in Jamul above a restaurant called the Haven. Jim could work for part of their rent after he got home from the base. Dianna was pregnant with their first baby. They kept the apartment until after their baby boy, Jamie was born on March 20, 1977.

Jim and Dianna Antoine, with first son, Jamie, 1977

The owners of the restaurant were very demanding of Jim's time so they found another apartment in El Cajon. It was closer to the base. Vicky moved in with them to share the rent. Our first grandchild, Jamie was a delight to all of the family, of course. He was perfect.

We had moved to California in Gina's senior year in high school. Jerry was a junior and Beth, a freshman. I felt bad that Gina had to change schools in her senior year but things like that happen. She did fine. The kids were always very good about the moves we made in life.

In May, 1977, after Gina graduated, she wanted to return to Rantoul, Illinois. She had already been promised her job back at the base chow hall in Rantoul. She was eighteen. She and her good friend, Mary Coonfare, got an apartment together.

Sometime in February of 1978, Gina called us. It was probably the hardest thing she had has ever had to do in this life. She was pregnant and wanted to come home. The father of the baby was in the Air Force but he did not want the baby or to get married. We could only thank God she had the strength to make that call and keep the baby. She and Dianna were both pregnant. They had each other to go through that time together. I am sure Dianna did not want to have another baby so soon either.

Dianna and Jim's second boy, Jeremy was born August 6, 1978 and Gina's boy, Joshua was born on September 12, 1978. Both were sweet and, of course, perfect. Jeremy did have a bit of a club foot, inherited from Jim.

It was not as bad a Jim's had been. Jer was in casting only a short time and the shoes were enough to correct the rest. As the boys grew, they were so different. Josh was the talker and Jer was the doer. Josh could talk his way out of anything and Jer could undo any lock around. Jamie was a bit more spoiled since he didn't have to share that first year and got so much attention from everyone. We all loved the babies, especially Gene. He thrived on being G-Pa. Our family was growing.

(Left to right) Jer, Jamie, Josh on "Ant Hill."

In June of 1978, Robert and Beva somehow got to bring David from Missouri to see Mom. He was waiting for his trial. I am not sure how Robert got a judge to let David go or what kind of bail was posted. I am sure it was because Robert was a Deputy Sheriff that made the difference. It was the last time Mom and David would ever see each other. With Mom being sick, there was no way she could ever make the trip back to Missouri. She died in April of 1980. David did have one last good time before he went to prison, thanks to Robert and Beva. We all went to Disneyland, Mexico, and Las Vegas with him. When they returned to Missouri, David was tried and given two life sentences. He would have to serve at least seven years on each. He was imprisoned for over fifteen years and paroled because he was a model prisoner. He became the head plumber at the prison and was the only inmate to be allowed outside the fence without a guard. When we visited him there, all the guards knew him and liked him. I truly believe if he had not been drinking he would never have done what he did but he did take the drink, committed the atrocity, and deserved the punishment. So many lives were changed because of his drinking that day. He was lucky that he got to live some of his life. The others were not that lucky.

Gina had met a young man on her return from Illinois, Lonnie Loya. Later, he would change his name back to his biological father's name of Polkinghorn. They met at Vicky's apartment in El Cajon, California. Lonnie was one of the many teenagers that hung out on Second Street in El Cajon on Friday and Saturday nights. Second Street was impassable because all the teenagers in El Cajon who had cars and wanted to show them off. They blocked the whole street just cruising driving up and down it. Lonnie had a Dodge Charger and he loved that car more than life itself.

The El Cajon Police let them do this because they knew where they all were so that it made their job easier. Most of them also hung out at Pizza Hut where Vicky was working. I guess that is how Gina and Lonnie got acquainted.

Lonnie wanted to marry Gina before the baby was born. Since I didn't know the biological father or had never even seen a picture of him, I asked them to wait.

Lonnie was very light skinned with blond hair. A typical Caucasian California boy. I worried if the baby had very dark hair or dark skin, it might have been harder for Lonnie to accept him. That turned out not to have ever entered Lonnie's mind. He had already accepted this baby as his own. No matter what, Josh was Lonnie's from the day he was born. I prevented Lonnie from being in the room at the moment of birth, which I am sorry for now.

Lonnie and Gina got married on April 6th, 1979 and had a very nice wedding at St Pius X church of Jamul. Gina made her own wedding dress. The wedding was perfect. We had the reception at the church and life was good. She and Lonnie found a small apartment in town.

Soon after Gina and Lonnie were married in 1979, they found out they were going to have another baby.

They found a small travel trailer for sale and asked if they could move it up onto our property. It was an older model, all real wood inside, very solid, and in good shape. We set it up beside the house and they moved in.

Lonnie, Gina & Joshua

Lonnie, Gina (Antoine) Polkinghorn, and children

It was not really an unselfish thing to do. Gene and I could use the help and it was good to have someone on the property if we were gone. Lonnie was just nineteen. I could only imagine how his mom felt about him and Gina getting married. They hardly knew Gina.

Beth had become close friends with another young girl named Annette Weller who lived on Mother Grundy Truck Trail. They went to high school together. Beth also got a job after school at Pizza Hut and the girls moved into Vicky's apartment in El Cajon.

Jerry finally came home from Illinois sometime in the summer of 1979. He was driving an old Dodge Super Bee with a motorcycle in the back seat. He didn't find his fortune in Illinois. He and Annette started dating when he returned from Illinois and were growing more serious about each other. He moved back into the house with us for a while. He and Annette later got married.

Annette, Dianna, Gina, Beth, Vicky

Sometime in September, 1979, Terry Swift called me and told me his wife Judy wanted a divorce. They had a little boy Nick in December, 1978. Judy was still in the Air Force and had Terry's ID taken away. He was forced off the base. She wasn't letting him see Nick.

This was before the kidnapping laws went into effect forbidding taking your own child out of the home. I suggested to Terry that he ask Judy to let him take Nick for a visit, then keep him and let her fight to get him back. Terry did manage to get Nick and had a plan. He and his friend Rick would leave Wyoming and come to our house in California.

When they arrived, they were a mess. Nick had a bad diaper rash but was otherwise healthy. He looked a little mal-nourished. His stomach looked extended. Could have been just the way Nick was built. He was a long and skinny kid. Terry's friend, Rick returned to his home while Terry and Nick stayed with us until Terry got a job and enough money to get an apartment.

Terry lived in fear for a while that Judy would send the police after him but she never even called. Judy knew Terry would come to us so I am sure she knew Nick was being cared for. Terry was a very good father.

(Left to right) Jo Ann, Gina, Jim, Vicky, and Terry Swift on Ant Hill

THE TRIP—1979

Gene and I went on a long, three month's trip in 1979. We had plenty of caretakers on the property now. We decided to visit everyone we had met in private life and in the service, all our old friends and family. We had no deadlines to meet. We would go where the road took us. We first went north to Merced, California to see Rick Mc Donald, one of Jim's friends from Chanute AFB.

Rick was an instructor on the B-1 bombers. I think the base was

Castle AFB. Rick gave Gene the royal tour of his school. It would always be one of Gene's special memories. The stealth bomber was very new then. Gene still missed the Air Force.

Then on to Spokane, Washington to see the McKees. It was the first time we had been with them since Germany. Bill had retired and was working for a dealership there. Then, we crossed the badlands of South Dakota, stopping at Mount Rushmore and on to Ellsworth, Wisconsin, Terry Odalen's home.

Terry had come to us in Germany as a friend of Keith Shields. We met Terry's family and got to see firsthand a sugar shack where maple syrup was made. The whole process from the sap of the tree to syrup. Something we had never seen before.

LAQUALLA SWEENY:

We then headed to Bear Creek, Wisconsin to visit Laqualla Sweeny. Laqualla was our God child. She came into our lives when we were stationed at Chanute AFB in Illinois in 1973. Laqualla's uncle, Tom Sweeny was an Air Force policeman at Chanute AFB. He and Jim had become good friends. One night Tom came to us very upset. His sister, a young runaway had been found dead in a bath tub in Memphis, Tennessee. She had just had a baby girl, Laqualla.

Tom wanted Jim to ride to Milwaukee, Wisconsin with him to get his mom and take her to Memphis to get the baby and identify his sister. Tom had no money and had a younger sister at home, Kristina, ten years old, who would need someone to stay with her. I said Jim could go with Tom since Tom's mom could not go with him.

The next time I heard from Tom's mom, the boys were in Memphis, Tennessee. The boys took a girlfriend of Tom's to go get the baby. The authorities would not release the baby to these juvenile kids. Jim called and told me they were with a really nice black family and were ok. I realized they were in the heart of the city of Memphis and this is not always the best place to be in in any big city. I called Tom's mom and told her I was going to wire her the bus money to go to Memphis and get those kids home. She said she couldn't leave Kristina. Then I told her Gene and I would drive to Milwaukee, seven hours by car. We would put her on a bus and bring Kristina home with us. Gene was shaking his head.

We went there, got Tom's mom on the bus, and took Kristina to our house. It all worked out. When the grandma, baby Laqualla, Tom, and Jim got back to our house with the baby, it was obvious she had black roots too. She was beautiful. In fact, Jim and Tom thought she was so beautiful he and Tom wrote a song for her. Not sure if Jim remembers it now.

The grandma wanted the baby baptized so we called our Chaplain at the base and he agreed to baptize her. We became her God parents and would stay in touch with Laqualla and her family until she graduated high school at age eighteen. She moved to Memphis to be part of her father's family, or at least the family of the man who claimed to be her father. Last we heard from her, she was still in Memphis and had a baby of her own.

From Bear Creek, Wisconsin, we went to Milwaukee to see Larry Jankowski. Larry was Father Larry, ordained in Rome at St. Peters. We met Larry when we were in Germany. He was studying in Rome and did some of his schooling at our base at Hahn, Germany. When Gene and I got to go to Rome, Larry took us to see Rome at night. The closest thing to Heaven is being in Rome and having your own tour guide. After serving as a priest for a very short time in Milwaukee, Larry met a woman struggling to raise her five kids alone. He left the priesthood to help her and they were married. This devastated his family but he stayed with Carol and helped to raise the children. They came one time to see us after our move to California. We wrote at Christmas for many years but finally lost touch. I think we were a reminder of the life he had before meeting Carol.

From Milwaukee, Wisconsin, we went to Chicago, Illinois to see our old friends, the Allots, Eileen and Chuck. Then we continued on to Chanute AFB in Rantoul, Illinois. Gene had to go back to his school and see how the base had changed. Some other friends were still there.

We went to visit the Hemmerichs who had become so close they were like family. From there, we went north to Syracuse, New York to see the Vanbodens. Vanboden had served with us and the McKees in Germany. He had watched our kids when we went to Rome with Bill and Zita.

After our stay in Syracuse, we went to Maine where our Chaplain from Germany, Father Whalen and his mom, were living. We had our first taste of lobster here at a place called Strawberry Hill, Maine. We went down the coast to see Niagara Falls, The Statue of Liberty and my favorite place, Ellis Island. Then we carried on to Washington D.C. and saw the Smithsonian Museums and all the sights.

On to Delaware to find Calloway. He had worked for Gene at Patrick AFB and spent most of his free time at our house. It was fun to see how he'd grown and changed from a young kid to a married man. We drove through the tunnel from Delaware to Norfolk, Virginia. I think it is the Chesapeake Bay tunnel and all underwater.

In Virginia, we stayed with Don and Evelyn Cockburn. Evelyn was my old friend Mary Ida's sister. My sister, Beva married her brother Robert. Evelyn was the one who came to take Mary and me home when we ran away. Don and Evelyn had also been with us in Germany but were stationed at a different base called Bitburg.

We then went to Ninety-Six, South Carolina to see the Corbins. You may remember, they were our next door neighbors in Alaska. They were now retired and Jack worked at a textile mill. He took us on a tour of at the mill. We saw the process from the raw cotton to the finished cloth. It was very noisy with lots of different machinery. Again, something we had never seen till then.

Then to Jacksonville, Florida to see the Ryans, Joyce and Ricky from the days in California before we were married. Ricky had retired from the Navy. He was a dietitian for a big hospital. He was still a sailor at heart. Great time always with these two.

North again to Kentucky and the Moutons. Our friendship with them would last till death do us part. Then to Nashville to see Gene's nephew, Ron Avis. Ron was driving the tour bus for Kenny Rogers then. He shared some of the excitement of his life style with us. Later, when Kenny had a throat problem, they actually left their buses in San Diego at the airport. Ron asked us to go and check on the buses to make sure they were safe there, which we did. When Ron and his fellow bus drivers came back to get the buses, we met them at the airport. They let all of us go aboard and ride back to El Cajon on the bus. It was a thrill for the kids. The buses were very plush inside with a scene painted on the outside of a big paddle-wheel gambling boat. Kenny was known for his song "The Gambler." Ron had a few of Kenny Rogers' souvenir shirts on the bus. He gave one to Gene and some of the kids. They were all thrilled to have them.

Antoine grandkids with Ron Avis, Kenny Rogers Tour Bus

From there on to St. Louis for our usual visits with family and friends; of course, stopping in Kimmswick and down at to the river at Hoppie's Marina. No trip would be complete without this.

From St. Louis to Wichita, Kansas, Rick Samples had retired and went to work in civil service. He was working here at the Boeing Aircraft plant as a quality control person. He gave us a VIP tour of their factory, seeing the construction of an aircraft from the ground up.

Finally we were headed west with a stopover in Tucson and then back home to California.

What a drive this had been. I made up my mind, it would be the last such trip. We would now see who came to visit us and those were the friends we would always go out of our way to see. We still keep touch with most of those we saw on that trip but only via email and exchanging Christmas catch up letters. We have grown closer to all those who did come to see us.

You can find me at the end of The Dirt Road.

Joann, Gene and Family at New York Wedding

❊ ❊ ❊

ABOUT THE AUTHOR

Phyllis Jo Ann Bainter was born in De Lassus, Missouri, August 20, 1935. The second child of six children, three boys and three girls. She was a very strong-willed girl some like to call it stubbornness or hard-headedness.

Her brother Jimmy died at eight months old from pneumonia. Her parents divorced when she was ten years old and her mother raised the children alone.

She met Eugene James Antoine in Kimmswick, Missouri in 1950. They were married on, 1 October 1955 and he would be the love of her life for 55 years. They had five children, Victoria Lynn, James Arthur, Eugenia Renee, Gerald William and Elizabeth Roseanne.

So far, there have been twenty grandchildren, two step-grandchildren, thirty-one great grandchildren and four step-great grandchildren. Seventeen of the grandchildren and their parents lived on the property owned by Gene and Jo Ann, for a good part of their lives. All twenty lived there at some time in their life. The homestead was called Ant Hill (for the first three letters of Antoine and because ants are so abundant, like the many number of children).

They all shared joy, survived illness, tragedy, good times and bad times. They made their own music, singing together and even had a family band called Greasewood, who played around the community and church for fifteen years. Love for God and family was always there.

Made in the USA
San Bernardino, CA
14 May 2020

71511286R00151